Open Minds

Open Minds

Exploring Global Issues through Reading and Discussion

Steven Widdows and Peter Voller

Ann Arbor

The University of Michigan Press

ISBN 0-472-08358-9
Library of Congress Catalog Card No. 96-60542
Published in the United States of America by
The University of Michigan Press
Manufactured in the United States of America

1999 1998 1997 1996 4 3 2 1

Contents

To the Student

By the time you start reading *Open Minds* you will probably have been learning English for several years and already will be able to read some texts. One of the purposes of *Open Minds* is to help you develop strategies for more effective reading. In fact "reading" is not just one skill but rather a set of related skills, such as looking out for specific information, seeing how ideas connect with one another, working out the meanings of unknown words, judging the intentions of the writer, and so on. These are the kinds of reading and vocabulary strategies that you will discover and practice in *Open Minds*.

Each unit of the book has two texts on the same theme, and each text has a task that you should do before you read the text and then other tasks that you should do after reading. Try to be aware of the point of doing any particular task. Which reading skill are you practicing? Do you think it is a good strategy to help you understand the text? You can check your ideas by looking at the table of reading and vocabulary skills that you will find at the end of this introduction. It shows you the skill practiced in each task. By doing this as you go through the book, you can decide for yourself which reading strategies seem useful to you. You could do the tasks on your own, but we think it is better to work on them together with a partner so that you can compare and discuss your answers. If you are doing the tasks without a teacher, you may also find the answer key at the end of each unit useful.

When you read the texts, do so without a dictionary and at a good pace. Do not worry about the words you do not recognize, but concentrate on following the main message of the text. We hope that you find the texts interesting, and we hope they will make you thoughtful too. The issues they discuss affect us all, and we hope that you will consider how the situation you are reading about relates to your own society and your own life.

Each unit has a set of fluency activities following the reading texts and tasks, so that you will have the opportunity to talk and listen to your classmates. The purpose of these activities is not just to recycle and expand the new words and information you have learned from the texts but also to encourage you to work out and express your beliefs, feelings, and ideas about the issues and to listen to what your classmates have to say. When you are doing these fluency activities, try not to be concerned about making language mistakes; accuracy is important in your overall English ability, but this is not the right time to concentrate on that aspect of your English skills. Remember, these are fluency activities.

Above all, enjoy *Open Minds* and let it be food for thought.

Reading and Vocabulary Skills

Contents	Task Type	Task Description
		Unit 1
Work and the Elderly		
Prereading		stating opinions
Task 1	global	choosing the best title
Task 2	global	skimming—true/false propositions
Task 3	intensive	cohesion—understanding referential words
Task 4	intensive	guessing questions
Task 5	vocabulary	word diamonds
Task 6	intensive	scanning —listing information
	response	using world knowledge
The Incredible Aging Woman		
Prereading		drawing inferences from photographs
Task 1	global	choosing the best summary of the text
Task 2	vocabulary	matching words and definitions
Task 3	intensive	scanning—listing information
Task 4	response	creative thinking/using world knowledge
Task 5	intensive	scanning—listing information
Task 6	response	drawing inferences from the text

Unit 2

Organic Vegetables

Prereading		activating world knowledge
Task 1	global	choosing the best summary of the text
Task 2	intensive	guessing questions
Task 3	global	matching people with their situations
Task 4	vocabulary	word diamonds
Task 5	response	brainstorming ideas/using world knowledge

Fast Food

Prereading		group survey
	vocabulary	matching words and definitions
		applying world knowledge to a table
Task 1	global	skimming—checking information
Task 2	global	deciding on truth level of text
Task 3	vocabulary	crossword puzzle
Task 4	intensive	scanning—listing information
Task 5	response	applying world knowledge to facts from the text
Task 6	response	brainstorming ideas/using world knowledge

Unit 3

Guano and Fishmeal

Prereading		activating world knowledge from a map
Task 1	global	choosing the best summary of the text
Task 2	global	ordering information chronologically
Task 3	vocabulary	word search—semantic grouping
Task 4	intensive	cohesion—understanding referential words
Task 5	response	brainstorming ideas/using world knowledge
Task 6	response	evaluating/brainstorming/using world knowledge

Bangladesh's Penny Bank

Prereading		applying world knowledge to a map
Prereading	vocabulary	brainstorming words
Task 1	global	ordering paragraph summaries
Task 2	intensive	scanning—completing a chart
Task 3	vocabulary	grouping words

Task 4	intensive	scanning—listing information
	response	using world knowledge
Task 5	response	thinking up questions to ask the subject of the text

Unit 4

High School Prom

Prereading	vocabulary	grouping words
Task 1	global	ordering paragraph summaries
Task 2	vocabulary	word search—matching words to definitions
Task 3	intensive	scanning—finding answers to questions
	response	drawing inferences from the text
Task 4	vocabulary	choosing appropriate words
	response	reacting to the subject of the text
Task 5	intensive	scanning—listing points in a chart
	response	using world knowledge
Task 6	response	predicting what happened next

Fear of the "Naturals"

Prereading		applying world knowledge to a table
Task 1	global	choosing the best summary of the text
Task 2	global	skimming—true/false propositions
Task 3	vocabulary	word search—dealing with unknown words
Task 4	intensive	scanning—listing points on six topics
Task 5	intensive	scanning—listing causes
	response	creative thinking/using world knowledge

Unit 5

The Want Makers

Prereading		activating world knowledge from a table
Task 1	global	skimming—ordering points from the text
Task 2	global	selecting main points
Task 3	intensive	cohesion—understanding referential words
Task 4	vocabulary	choosing correct definitions in context
Task 5	response	brainstorming ideas/using world knowledge

The Hidden Persuaders

Prereading		discussing advertisements
Task 1	global	choosing the best opening paragraph
Task 2	intensive	guessing questions
Task 3	intensive	scanning—completing a chart
Task 4	vocabulary	word search—semantic grouping
Task 5	response	using world knowledge/expressing opinions

Unit 6

Murder in the Rain Forest

Prereading	vocabulary	brainstorming words
Task 1	global	skimming—true/false propositions
Task 2	intensive	sentence completion
Task 3	vocabulary	word search—matching definitions
Task 4	intensive	completing a flowchart
Task 5	response	brainstorming ideas/using world knowledge
Task 6	response	predicting possibilities

Cleaner Cars for California

Prereading		group survey
Task 1	global	ordering paragraph summaries
Task 2	global	selecting main points
Task 3	intensive	simplifying text
Task 4	vocabulary	crossword puzzle
Task 5	response	explaining false reasoning
Task 6	response	analyzing the writer's attitudes

Unit 7

Racial Equality at Work

Prereading		brainstorming ideas from world knowledge
Task 1	global	skimming—true/false propositions
Task 2	vocabulary	matching words and definitions
Task 3	intensive	simplifying text
Task 4	response	imagining how people felt
Task 5	response	brainstorming ideas/using world knowledge

Asians in Australia

Prereading	vocabulary	word association
Prereading		predicting mood of the text
Task 1	global	selecting main points
Task 2	intensive	guessing questions
Task 3	intensive	cohesion—understanding referential words
Task 4	vocabulary	word diamonds
Task 5	intensive	matching subjects with their situations
Task 6	response	comparing the text with your own situation

Unit 8

Bored Out of Life

Prereading	vocabulary	reacting to a photograph
Task 1	global	selecting main points
Task 2	vocabulary	crossword puzzle
Task 3	intensive	scanning—completing a chart
Task 4	global	skimming—true/false propositions
Task 5	response	brainstorming ideas/using world knowledge

World Evil with Its Roots in the North-South Divide

Prereading		applying world knowledge to a map
Text Task	response	predicting the next part of the text
Task 1	global	choosing the best conclusion
Task 2	global	ordering information chronologically
Task 3	vocabulary	word search—dealing with unknown words
Task 4	intensive	scanning—listing new information
	response	reacting to new information

Unit 9

Inside a Third World City

Prereading	vocabulary	brainstorming words
Task 1	global	choosing a summary of the text
Task 2	global	understanding the writer's attitude
Task 3	vocabulary	matching words and definitions
Task 4	vocabulary	scanning text for synonyms

Task 5	intensive	scanning—completing a chart
	response	using world knowledge to add to chart
Task 6	response	brainstorming ideas/using world knowledge

Inside an English City

Prereading		activating world knowledge
Task 1	global	ordering paragraph summaries
Task 2	intensive	guessing questions
Task 3	vocabulary	grouping words
Task 4	intensive	deciding writer's beliefs
Task 5	intensive	distinguishing facts and opinions
Task 6	response	thinking up questions
Task 7	response	brainstorming ideas/using world knowledge

Unit 10

Woman's Work Is Never Done

Prereading		expressing and explaining opinions
Task 1	global	ordering paragraph summaries
Task 2	vocabulary	word search—semantic grouping
Task 3	intensive	cohesion—referential words
Task 4	vocabulary	matching words and definitions
Task 5	global	deciding on truth level of text

Who's That Man?

Prereading		expressing opinions about photographs
Task 1	global	choosing the best summary
Task 2	global	skimming—true/false propositions
Task 3	vocabulary	word search—semantic grouping
Task 4	intensive	rewriting and simplifying topic sentences
Task 5	vocabulary	word search—dealing with unknown words
Task 6	response	creative thinking/using world knowledge

To the Teacher

Brief Description

Open Minds is a speaking/reading skills textbook for adult and young adult ESL and EFL students who have reached at least an intermediate level of proficiency. It offers integrated practice to develop reading and oral fluency skills and to increase learners' awareness both of language, specifically reading strategies, and of the sociocultural context within which English and their native tongues are used. *Open Minds* can therefore help learners to find their own *voices* in English by helping them to evaluate authentic texts in English and to discuss these texts and the themes that they develop in terms of their own values. This combination of cognitive and affective tasks and activities is designed not only to promote language acquisition but also to raise learners' awareness of themselves as members of both a language community and a larger society.

The ten units should take between 40 and 60 hours of class time to complete, depending on how you choose to treat the materials. Each unit consists of two separate texts on a common theme, each with a set of reading development tasks. The texts lead on to a set of fluency activities on the same theme. The themes have been chosen to help learners become more aware of and to express their opinions about current social and environmental issues. Some of the themes are controversial, and reading and thinking about such topics, we believe, if handled sensitively by the teacher, act as a powerful stimulus to discussion. The titles and themes of the units are as follows:

Unit 1	The Remains of the Day	old age
Unit 2	Our Daily Bread	nutrition
Unit 3	For Whose Benefit?	aid and development
Unit 4	Glad to Be Gay?	homosexuality
Unit 5	The Dream Sellers	advertising
Unit 6	Biosphere Blues	ecology and the environment
Unit 7	Pride and Prejudice	minority rights

Unit 8	Out of Our Minds	drug abuse
Unit 9	Dead End Street	poverty
Unit 10	Guys 'n' Dolls	gender roles

Apparatus

Open Minds is a workbook, which students are expected to write in, thus providing a record of what they are learning. Its use is self-explanatory: an answer key has been provided at the end of each unit so that it can be used for self-study; additional notes at the end of each unit are provided for the teacher. The symbol 🕮 in the text will alert the teacher to these notes.

Outstanding Features

Prereading tasks warm learners up to the theme and activate their schemata.
Maps and photos are included to stimulate interest and provide paralinguistic support.
Texts are adapted from authentic sources.
Tasks are designed to teach learners to read English in the same way as native speakers and to raise their awareness of reading strategies so that they are better equipped to choose appropriate techniques when reading in the future.
Reading tasks develop global, intensive, vocabulary-building and response strategies systematically.
Most of the reading tasks can be done either in pairs/groups or individually (and therefore as self-study); fluency activities all involve pair and group work.
Fluency activities help learners to acquire language through a process of assimilating what they have learned from the texts, combining it with their own knowledge, and expressing this in the activities.
Fluency activities involve learners' personal experience and world knowledge.
Fluency activities encourage learners to explore and reassess their own values and thus find their own *voices* in English.

How to Use the Texts and Reading Tasks

Each of the ten units consists of two authentic reading texts each with a set of prereading and reading tasks. The first reading text is generally at a simpler lexical and syntactic level than the second. The texts come from a variety of English-speaking countries, and, although not culture-bound (indeed the subject matter covers a diversity of cultural and social milieus), they are not culturally neutral, for they were all written for specific, literate, and educated audiences. However, when dealing with culture-specific texts, the reading tasks provide opportunities for learners to compare the situation reported in the text with that prevailing in their own cultures. Also, the topics of the units have been chosen because they are of world-wide relevance.

Prereading Materials

The prereading materials are designed to arouse interest in the topics and to activate learners' schemata, more specifically their existing world knowledge and language schemata. Before doing the prereading tasks students should be asked to guess what the unit will be about from its title and to predict the content of each text from its title. Students should read through a text quickly and without using a dictionary: we suggest that students should look over task 1 before starting to read a text in order to give their reading some direction.

Reading Tasks

The text-related tasks will help learners to understand different aspects of the text while at the same time raising their awareness of the various component skills of reading. The overall arrangement of the tasks gives learners systematic practice in global and intensive reading and vocabulary-building strategies. Within this framework, the skills practiced in individual tasks vary widely because this will help to show learners that appropriate reading strategies will vary according to the text and one's purpose in reading it. A table laying out the main reading and vocabulary skills underlying each task is provided elsewhere in this introductory material so that the strategies involved in reading a text can be made explicit to students. The tasks vary to suit the text but can be classified as follows:

prereading tasks, involving prediction or learners' existing knowledge of the topic, which prepare them for reading the text and place it in a recognizable context;

global reading tasks that enable learners to see the text as a whole, thus grasping the writer's intentions and methods;

intensive reading tasks that cover a variety of skills such as searching for specific information, identifying cohesive devices, and sequencing;

vocabulary tasks that not only help learners to broaden their vocabularies in topic-related domains but also encourage them to form strategies for dealing with new words;

response tasks that allow learners to react to the content and intent of a text and prepare them to go beyond it into the fluency activities.

Further Suggestions

It is worth stressing the flexible nature of these reading materials: the different level of complexity between the first and the second text in each unit means that learning activities can be tailored for mixed ability classes. If classroom time is short, the answer key allows learners to read the texts as self-study materials outside the classroom, although we would recommend that at least the prereading tasks be done in class in order to prepare learners for the reading experience, and that feedback activities on the texts be done in class before embarking on the fluency activities. Also, if a self-access mode of learning is used, it would be better for learners to go through the tasks in pairs, so that they can compare answers with one another as well as with the answer key.

How to Use the Fluency Activities

In the fluency activities the emphasis shifts to speaking and (by default) listening. These activities are designed to engross learners intellectually and affectively. They cover a wide range of task types, including information-gap activities of various personal, opinion, and cognitive kinds, brainstorming, ranking, evaluating, problem solving, values clarification, creative thinking, and experiential activities. The title of each activity usually indicates the kind of task involved.

Project Activities

The last two activities of each unit consist of a project and a debate (except in unit 3 where the Trading Game replaces the debate). The purpose of the project activities is to get learners to go outside the classroom in order to gather information that they then share with their classmates. The information gathering can be done individually or in pairs and can be done in English or in the student's first language, but the presentation and sharing of information in class must be done in English. The purpose of these project activities is both to help learners to find their own *voice* in English and to help them to realize that what they are studying is not a separate compartment labeled English but a subject that interconnects with their lives beyond the classroom. Ways in which project information can be shared in class are suggested in the notes to the teacher and include poster presentations, short talks, or less formal means of information sharing. It is really up to individual teachers to decide how formal these activities should be and how much time to devote to them.

Debate Activities

The same applies to the debate activities, which could be organized quite formally with main and subsidiary speakers for and against the motion. An alternative, less time-consuming, and less anxiety-raising way of having a "debate" is as follows.

split the class into two (if the class is large, subdivide into smaller groups), one for and one against the proposition;

get the two sides, either individually or in small groups, to brainstorm ideas, share them, and note down all possible arguments in favor of their motion;

organize the two sides into a dyadic circle (two circles, one inside the other) so that supporters of the motion are matched face to face against supporters of the opposite point of view;

each person starts arguing his or her case with the person facing him/her, point counter point;

every few minutes have the outer circle rotate to the left so that students get to argue with a succession of partners;

after 15–20 minutes stop the activity, have a feedback session (what were the best arguments for and against, who were the best arguers and why, what were the easy and difficult parts of the debate, and so on), and hold a vote on the motion according to what people really believe.

(We learned this way of debating from David Gregory.)

Classroom Organization

Various configurations are possible, but we recommend that text-related activities be done in pairs or threes, and fluency activities should always be done in small groups unless otherwise specified. If you have classes of very mixed levels of proficiency, you may think it wiser to have the weaker students work on just the first reading text (which is simpler and shorter than the second) while the more proficient students work through the second text too and then have the more advanced students explain the gist of the second text to the others. The students at a lower level of proficiency could then study the second text in self-access mode.

Time Needed

Obviously this will vary depending on such factors as class size and level of proficiency but, as a very rough guide, expect the two texts plus reading tasks to take up to two hours, while the fluency activities as far as the project and debate will take an additional hour. The project and debate together will take at least forty minutes and could take much longer depending on how deeply you want to go into them.

Teacher's Role

As teacher your role is one of classroom manager and participant observer. You should be prepared to introduce the topic; to organize the class; to check progress on the reading tasks and provide assistance and answers; to monitor the fluency activities and participate in them in a nondirective way; to assist learners with useful language and vocabulary; and to organize feedback at the end of each fluency activity. The feedback sessions are important, both to help you observe and to help learners consolidate their learning experience. As oral fluency is the focus of the activities, teachers should refrain from correcting learners' language errors when they are speaking.

Unit 1
The Remains of the Day

Work and the Elderly

Prereading

Which of the following statements about old people do you believe? Check [√] your answers.

	Agree	Don't Know	Disagree
They can't keep up with modern changes.			
They know how to use computers.			
They are good at sorting out business problems.			
They do not contribute much to the economy.			
They are easily trained for high-tech jobs.			
They are often absent from work because of illness.			

Compare your answers. Do they give a positive image of old people or a rather negative one? Now read the text. Does it question any of your ideas?

Reading

Look at task 1 below and then read through the text quickly, without using a dictionary.

Despite laws against age discrimination, older workers in the United States are frequently victims when firms reduce their workforces. But the stereotype of the older worker who can't keep up with changing times is being disproved, both on the job and in a new study out today.

This is the nerve center of a nationwide hotel chain that employs a group of senior citizens to take charge of its computer sales and bookings; and they are not alone. At **its** Connecticut office, the third largest insurance company in America employs a team of retirees as troubleshooters for its customers. It is a **trend** that may change the job market of the nineties. Older Americans are coming back to work, and a study released today claims that hiring them is not only helping the individuals, it is also good for the business.

"If we were able to put **those people** to work," says Thomas Moloney of the Commonwealth Fund, "we'd have a hundred and ninety billion dollar increase in our economic output per year, at a time when we desperately need that."

Research on job performance of employees over fifty-five at three different corporations that have made hiring the elderly company policy shows that older workers can be easily trained for high-tech jobs, are flexible about work schedules, have lower absenteeism and lower turnover than the young, and are often better salespeople.

"**We** tend to think about older people in terms of long-term care and the effects they're having on the high cost of health-care services," says economist Michael Barin, "whereas there are millions and millions of older people who are healthy and want to work, and what we found in our studies is that they are productive, active people."

Like Mary Seymour, at eighty-three. She insists that a nineteen hour workweek at the insurance company where she has worked for sixty years keeps her youthful. "I really like working. I think if **you** stay home all the time life soon gets dull."

Research shows that there are now over six million older Americans ready and willing to return to work. Ironically, analysts say, the biggest barriers to hiring them are federal laws. If you are over sixty-five and go back to work, you will probably lose all Medicare benefits and most social security benefits once your salary goes above ninety-seven hundred dollars a year. But America's changing population may force a change in laws. The labor pool of skilled young people is rapidly shrinking, and so some people believe that before long many employers will have no choice but to turn to their parents, even grandparents, to lend a helping hand.

Task 1

Choose the best title for the text and give your reason for choosing it.

"Reasons for and against Employing the Elderly"
"Old Age: A Waste of Human Resources"
"Can Older Workers Save America?"
"Older Workers Improve their Performance"

Task 2

Which of the following statements are true [T], that are false [F], and that are not answered in the text [NA]? Mark your answer in the brackets.

[ ] It is difficult for an employer to fire older workers because the law protects them.
[ ] Older people are more reliable and flexible workers.
[ ] One problem with hiring older people is retraining them for high-tech computer jobs.
[ ] More elderly people would work if they didn't lose their federal benefits.
[ ] The number of old people in long-term health care is outnumbered by those who are healthy and want to work.
[ ] More and more old people will probably be employed in the future because of the shortage of young skilled workers.

Adapted from a report by Doug Tunnell for CBS News, Miami, April / May, 1991.

Task 3

What do the following words, printed in **bold** in the text, refer to?

This (para. 2)
its (para. 2)
trend (para. 2)
those people (para. 3)
we (para. 5)
you (para. 6)

Task 4

Write questions for these answers.

a hundred and ninety billion dollars
it was carried out by corporations that have a policy of hiring the elderly
because she doesn't want to lead a dull life
fear of losing medical and social security benefits

Task 5

a. Complete the following sentences by putting one word from the text into each of the blanks. The letters of the three words are jumbled in the diamond.

I
CR
PRI
SOBLL
FEELE
EEY
TX
I

1. ____________ is another word for senior citizens. (para. 2)
2. A plan or program that has been decided by a company (or a government) is called a ____________. (para. 4)
3. If you can adapt easily to circumstances as they change, you are ____________. (para. 4)

b. Now do the same for the following three sentences.

E
DPI
OUBLE
RUNREDT
TRORSO
VOHOT
RVS
E

1. The ____________ of people in a company is the rate at that they leave it and are replaced by new people. (para. 4)
2. If an idea is ____________, it is shown to be untrue. (para. 1)
3. A ____________ is a person employed by a company to solve difficulties. (para. 2)

Task 6

How many reasons for employing older people can you find in the text. List them. Can you think of any others?

The Incredible Aging Woman

Prereading

Look at these two pictures and use your imagination to answer the following questions.

How old are they? Are they related? What kinds of things does each of them enjoy doing? How many friends do they have? What is each of them planning to do in the future?

Tell your partner your answers.

Reading

Look at task 1 below and then read through the text quickly, without using a dictionary.

In an amazing three-year experiment, Pat Moore lived as an elderly woman on the streets of New York City. As "Old Pat" she went around trying to find out what it was like to be old. During the unusual experiment Pat was shortchanged by shopkeepers, verbally abused when she got in the way, and assaulted and left for dead by a gang of youths out for drug money. She considered the attack a minor event. It was overshadowed by feelings of loneliness and frustration as she found that those who treated "Young Pat" so well were condescending, aggressive, and only too willing to deceive Old Pat.

Typically, a clerk in a Manhattan stationery store ignored Old Pat. He shouted at her when she asked if he sold typewriter ribbons, and, when she genuinely misheard his question about what kind of typewriter she owned, he yelled out her mistake to humiliate her.

Pat would return to the same store the next day as her young self, with shoulder-length blond hair, young tanned skin, and often the same cheap print dress as Old Pat—not that anyone ever noticed. In the stationery shop the next day, Young Pat did exactly the same things, even making the same mistake. This time, however, the clerk just laughed and made a friendly reply.

Verbal abuse was upsetting, but she also had to watch out for people taking physical advantage of her. Being shortchanged and being physically outmaneuvered in a waiting line were commonplace. And, as time went on, she found herself becoming more and more submissive. "I became so intimidated by the attitude of others, by the fact that they would be so exasperated with me. I started to move aside to let people pass and began to say to myself, after all, old ladies have plenty of time, don't they?"

To ensure that her own ill-treatment was not just a by-product of New York, Old Pat traveled to 116 American cities. She looked for differences in attitude between small and large towns, between different nationalities. She found none.

As she empathized more and more with Old Pat she found new friends among the elderly. She "came out" to a discreet circle of elderly women. They took her shopping, advised her on what situations to try out and what to avoid. As far as the disguise was concerned, though, the clothes were the easy part.

Despite the success of the disguise, Pat Moore continually felt guilty that she could change back to being Young Pat. "I was always painfully aware the disguise was just a shell for me." To her surprise, however, when she voiced this guilt to her elderly friends, they confirmed the feeling. They too felt that they were in a shell—young minds trapped behind old faces.

This discovery was a turning point for her. It confirmed her in the growing knowledge that the elderly weren't handicapped by their own physical disabilities so much as by the attitudes and psychological barriers set up by others.

Advertisers must take the blame for a lot of the attitudinal problems in society, says Pat Moore. "Advertising treats the young as the only consumers, and it shows invariably that mythic creature, the perfect user, when in reality we all go through periods of lessened ability—when we are young or sick." She will only be happy when advertising reflects the view that "there are no elderly, only people older than ourselves, and there are no disabled, only differently abled people."

One of Old Pat's fondest memories is meeting a six-year-old boy on the beach who chatted to her as a friend and an equal. The child responded to her naturally and without hesitation, because he didn't know any better.

Adapted from an article by Lucie Young in the *Guardian*, 1 August 1989, 17.

Task 1

Which of these is the best summary of the text?

a. However many bad things happen to old people, there are always some good things to make life seem better.

b. The experiences of Old Pat and Young Pat were very different. As a result, Pat was able to learn a lot about people's attitudes toward the elderly.

c. The attitude that most people have toward the elderly is directly related to the way in which advertising creates false images of society.

Task 2

Match these words with their definitions.

shortchanged	dishonestly take advantage of
assaulted	frightened and threatened
deceive	extremely annoyed and frustrated
humiliate	physically attacked
intimidated	given back less than enough money
exasperated	make someone feel ashamed and stupid
verbally abuse	say unkind, cruel, or rude words

Task 3

What were the bad things and the good things that happened to Pat when she was "Old Pat"? List them.

Good Things	Bad Things

Task 4

How do you think Pat disguised herself? What kinds of things would she have had to do to make herself look and act like an old woman? Write your answers.

Her face	
Her body	
Her legs	
Her hands	
Her teeth	
Her voice	
Her hearing	
Her sight	

Task 5

What did Pat learn from the experiment? List your ideas.

Other people's attitudes toward the elderly:

Old people's feelings:

Advertising and the elderly:

Task 6

Why was it that the child whom Old Pat met on the beach was able to respond to her? What didn't he "know any better"?

Fluency Activities

Perceptions

a. How old is old? At what age do we start and finish different phases of our lives? Note down your answers for these people.

	From	To
A child		
An adolescent		
A young adult		
A middle-aged person		
An old person		

Which phase are you in? Which phase is the most enjoyable? Why? Compare your answers with other people in your group. Have you all chosen similar ages? If not, why not?

b. Your teacher is going to dictate some sentences to you. After writing each sentence note down how old you think the subject of each sentence is.

	Age
1.	
2.	
3.	
4.	
5.	
6.	

Compare what you've written and discuss any important differences.

Associations

Which of the following words do you connect with youth and which with old age?

lonely	slim	childish
mature	ambitious	active
open-minded	bad-tempered	fashionable
worn out	fresh	sexy
tanned	wrinkles	studying
going gray	responsible	naughty
false teeth	dirty	athletic

Look at the words in your "youth" group. Why do you associate these words with youth? Can you think of reasons why any of them should *not* apply to older people?

Survey

Check [√] the items that you expect to be serious problems for elderly people.

[ ] fear of crime
[ ] poor health
[ ] not having enough money to live on
[ ] loneliness
[ ] not having enough medical care
[ ] not feeling needed
[ ] not having enough to do to keep busy
[ ] not having enough friends
[ ] not having enough job opportunities
[ ] poor housing
[ ] not having enough clothing

Compare your answers.

This survey was conducted on 4,250 people in the United States. Your teacher will show you the results that were obtained from over-65s and from the rest. Are the class's answers closer to the over-65s or the rest? Why is there such a difference between old people's experience and younger people's perceptions?

Interview

Imagine that you are interviewing an elderly person. What questions would you ask? In groups, make up a list of interesting questions.

Go out and interview an old person, and report back to your class next week.

Imagination

What kind of society would you like to live in when you are older? Note down the changes that will have to occur to bring this about.

Project

Look at some advertisements on TV and in newspapers and magazines. How are old people used in these advertisements? What kinds of ads are aimed at old people? Which ads exclude them?

Report your findings back to the class, bringing some examples if you can.

Debate

Divide yourselves into two teams (For and Against) and brainstorm as many arguments as you can. Then either split up your arguments among the team and each side take turns presenting and defending your case, or pair off with a member of the opposing team and argue it out face to face. Argue either for or against the following statement.

Older people are a burden on society.

Teacher's Notes and Answer Key

Work and the Elderly

Prereading. Did anyone answer as follows? Disagree, Agree, Agree, Disagree, Agree, Disagree. These would suggest a very positive and informed view of older people and their abilities.

Task 1. "Old Age: A Waste of Human Resources," because it summarizes one of the main points of the text. "Can Older Workers Save America?" is also good because it places the report in context and asks a rhetorical question. The other two titles are misleading and dull.

Task 2. F, T, F, T, NA, T

Task 3. This = nerve center of a hotel chain; *its* = the third largest insurance company in America; *trend* = employing retirees; *those people* = older Americans; *we* = the public (or we economists); *you* = people in general

Task 4. Suitable questions are the following.

How much would America's economic output increase if older people went to work?
Who carried out research on the job performance of employees over fifty-five?
Why does Mary continue working?
What prevents many over-65s from going back to work?

Task 5. a. 1. retirees; 2. policy; 3. flexible
b. 1. turnover; 2. disproved; 3. troubleshooter

Task 6. At least six: it would increase the economic output of the United States by $190 billion; older workers can be easily trained for high-tech jobs; they are flexible about work schedules; they have lower absenteeism and lower turnover than the young; they are often better salespeople. Another reason might be that it would cut back on health-care costs: people get bored and sick when they are stuck at home.

The Incredible Aging Woman

Task 1. The best summary is c.

Task 2. shortchanged = given back less than enough money; *assaulted* = physically attacked; *deceive* = dishonestly take advantage of; *humiliate* = make someone feel ashamed and stupid; *intimidated* = frightened and threatened; *exasperated* = extremely annoyed and frustrated; *verbally abuse* = say unkind, cruel, or rude words

Task 4. Face: latex mask, face powder, wig, and glasses; *Body:* a wrap to stop her standing upright and to give her a slight humpback; *Legs:* small splints of balsa wood at the back of each knee to restrict flexion, tight tube of material around thighs to keep legs close together and prevent walking fast; *Hands:* tape around fingers and gloves to make bending difficult and to simulate arthritis; *Teeth:* a paste of crayon and oil to stain them; Voice: gargling with salt and water for several minutes to make her voice raspy for six hours; *Hearing:* high density wax in the ears to impair hearing; *Sight:* baby oil in the eyes to cloud her vision

Fluency Activities

Perceptions. b. Dictate six statements to the class that begin with either He (or she) is too young to . . . or He (or she) is too old to . . . . Suitable statements would be: understand love, get married, cry, go to a disco, die, get in a fight, own a company, be a student, learn a new language, change jobs, etc.

Associations. It may be necessary to point out that students need not group all the words in the list if they feel that a word is not particularly associated with either youth or old age.

Survey. If possible project the following table on an overhead projector (OHP).

	A%	B%
Fear of crime	23	50
Poor health	21	51
Not having enough money to live on	15	62
Loneliness	12	60
Not having enough medical care	10	44
Not feeling needed	7	54
Not having enough to do to keep busy	6	37
Not having enough friends	5	28
Not having enough job opportunities	5	45
Poor housing	4	35
Not having enough clothing	3	16

A = percentage of the elderly who experience these as serious problems
B = percentage of other adults who expect these to be serious problems for the elderly
(*Source*: Harris and Associates 1975 as reported in Mike O'Donnell *Age and Generation*, [London: Tavistock Publications Ltd., 1988].)

Interview. Students can interview old people in their first language (L1), as long as they report back in English. One purpose of these project activities is to break down the barriers between L1 and second language (L2) use.

Unit 2
Our Daily Bread

Organic Vegetables—Paying Extra for Chemical-Free Produce

Prereading

Make a list of what you usually eat for breakfast. Which of these foods would your grandparents have eaten when they were your age? What does this tell us about the way food production and consumption have changed in the last fifty years?

Reading

Look at task 1 below and then read through the text quickly, without using a dictionary.

"We've been buying organic vegetables for about 15 years now—for as long as they've been around," says a customer as he weighs the organic broccoli that he has just selected here at Bread & Circus, a natural food store in Boston. The price is $1.98 per pound; conventionally grown broccoli is 50 cents less per pound. "But this is natural," says the retired carpenter. "It doesn't really cost that much more. At the end of the year, $15, $20, maybe $25 at the most. It isn't really that much. You don't need all those chemicals," he says, leaning forward to whisper his point. "Besides, they get into our water."

Turning to organic produce for both personal and environmental reasons is a growing trend. In 1976 vegetable grower Paul Harlow began to make his 60 acres of Vermont farmland chemical free. Harlow grows vegetables—carrots, cabbage, squash, kale. He and his father were troubled by the way the soil looked after farming for two decades with the commercial fertilizers and pesticides. "It just seemed like our soil had less organic matter," recalls Harlow. "There weren't any earthworms. We saw a lot of weeds we hadn't seen before." It took about 10 years, says Harlow, before the land came back "into a natural balance." Harlow had to learn special cultivation techniques, including spacing and rotating crops to balance what is put back into and extracted from the soil.

To kill insect pests, Harlow relies on natural predators like ladybugs. For fertilizer, he uses "green manure" (from plants) and cattle manure, which he buys. Controlling weeds is the most costly aspect of organic farming, he says. "I spend between $600 and $800 an acre just for hand-weeding," Harlow says. "A chemical farmer could probably do that for $25 worth of spray and not a lot of time."

But Harlow is satisfied. The earthworms are back, and he doesn't have to be concerned that his two children are exposed to hazardous chemicals in the barn or in the fields, where they sometimes eat carrots straight from the ground. Despite higher costs, says Harlow, "I have to believe the yields are just as good as the chemical farmer's down the road."

But not all farmers are convinced that organic growing is practical. Jim Wilson, who farms in Lexington, Mass., where produce is sold directly to customers, uses a "systems approach" to pest management—lessening but not eliminating chemicals. "I don't believe that at this time, with the variety of vegetables that our customers demand, that it's possible," says Wilson. "We grow 41 different items, 35 of which are never sprayed with pesticides. Vegetables like tomatoes spoil quickly if there's too much rain and they haven't been protected by fungicides. Composting is supplemented with chemical fertilizer."

If there's a way to help increase the supply, suggests Jim Pierce, a staff scientist at Environmental Action in Washington D.C., it's to help farmers monetarily during a three-year conversion period from chemical to organic farming. During this period, crop productivity drops. But when the conversion is complete, yields go back up. "We ought to restructure the [U.S. government's agricultural] subsidy program," says Pierce, whose job includes developing alternatives to pesticides, "so that when the farmer makes this conversion . . . he doesn't go under financially."

"The agrichemical business is a huge and very powerful industry . . . ," says Pierce, "and legislators are reluctant to adopt measures that are detrimental to the agricultural chemical industry."

Task 1

Which of these is the best summary of the text?

a. Growing and eating organic vegetables, even though they cost more, are becoming more popular because the vegetables are grown without using chemicals.

Adapted from an article by Elizabeth A. Brown in the *Christian Science Monitor*, 7 July 1989.

b. More and more farmers and consumers are going organic in spite of the efforts of agrichemical companies to stop the spread of organic farms.
c. Organic farming is better for the land but raises costs for both farmers and consumers and is not practical for all vegetables.
d. Opinions vary about the value of organic farming, and farmers need more government support if they are to convert from chemical farming.

Task 2

Write questions for these answers.

$15–25 more per year
organic matter decreased and earthworms disappeared
natural predators, "green manure" and cattle manure
because they spoil quickly in wet weather
because their crop productivity drops

Task 3

Make six sentences by matching the subjects (A) with what the text says about them (B):

A	B
The carpenter	can play safely on the farm
Harlow	wants the government to help farmers go organic
His children	are under pressure from big business interests
Wilson	now uses no chemicals whatsoever
Pierce	still uses pesticides on certain vegetables
Legislators	doesn't mind paying more for organic vegetables

Task 4

a. Complete the following sentences by putting one word from the text into each of the blanks. The letters of the three words are jumbled in the diamond.

L
MEN
UVAIN
RENTER
MONEY
LID
A

1. An ____________ issue is one connected to the natural world we live in.
2. ____________ is animal dung used as fertilizer.
3. The ____________ of an area of land is how much food it produces.

b. Now do the same for the following three sentences.

I
HAD
MIRED
TARZAN
SOUSE
LOT
L

1. The ____________ is the top layer of earth that plants can grow in.
2. Something that is ____________ is dangerous to your health or safety.
3. If something is ____________ it causes harm or damage.

Task 5

In what ways could the agrichemical business influence legislators against organic farming? List your ideas.

Fast Food

Prereading

a. Ask a classmate the following questions. Get together with other classmates and see how similar and different your answers are.

Group Survey on Fast Food
What is fast food?
How often do you eat fast food? ☐ every day ☐ about once a week ☐ very occasionally ☐ never
What do you like/dislike about fast food?

b. Match the words with the explanations:

Calories	a substance under the skin
Protein	substances that provide the body with energy
Carbohydrates	the amount of energy that a food will produce
Fat	substances that help the body grow
Vitamins	substances present in the earth that are essential to plant and animal life
Minerals	substances found in food that keep you healthy

c. Look at the table in the text below. Does it describe a well-balanced meal that satisfies our need for energy and nutrients? What information does this table fail to give us?

Reading

Look at task 1 below and then read through the text quickly, without using a dictionary.

Fast food companies are well aware of their image as sellers of "junk food," and much of their advertising budget is spent trying to dispel this image. Health and good living are the favorite themes, and one tactic is to mystify us with the details of the wonderful vitamins and essential minerals they pack into every item they sell. On the surface their glossy pamphlets can look very impressive. The company's product appears to contain vast quantities of nutrients necessary for a balanced diet and healthy life.

Of course, no one denies that foods such as meat, bread, milk, and potatoes are a useful part of a balanced diet. But these foods can be diluted in a typical fast food meal, with calories added in the form of fat, sugar, or refined carbohydrates. The density of the nutrients will then be lower, which means consuming more calories to get enough of the other essentials. The table below is an example of one company's analysis of "a typical meal combination."

These figures show how much the product can fulfill the recommended needs of an adult and of a child. The careful reader will see that neither adult nor child is especially well served. In both cases a greater proportion of daily energy needs (the calories) is supplied by this meal than are the needs for any

Analysis of a "Typical Meal"	Percentage of Daily Requirements for		
large hamburger, french fries, apple pie, regular cola		Average Adult	Average Child 5–14 years
Fat: 64.4 grams	Energy	51%	62%
	Protein	53%	65%
Protein: 32.9 grams	Vitamins		
	A	5%	8%
Energy: 1,283 calories	C	19%	26%
	B_1	42%	53%
Sodium: 1,488 milligrams	Minerals		
	calcium	44%	34%
Carbohydrates: 152.7 grams	iron	34%	32%

of the three vitamins, calcium, and iron. The meal gives half the daily calorie need of an adult, and nearly two-thirds the daily calorie need of a "child aged 5 to 14." Yet the meal does not supply anything near half or two-thirds of the daily need for vitamin A or vitamin C, and the figures for iron and calcium are not so impressive, especially for children. All these nutrients would have to be found in other foods eaten during the day to make up for the low levels in this meal. If the eater is not to get seriously overweight, then he or she would have to find the nutrients in foods that did not have another high dose of calories.

A second point a careful reader will also note is what is *not* included in the table. The meal is short, for example, in vitamin B_2, providing less than 20% of the child's needs. On the other hand, the fat content is 64.4 grams, providing about 45% of the calories, which is well above the 30–35% of calories from fat that the Department of Health recommends. Worse still, the meal contains a heavy dose of saturated fat. Some of this may be from the meat, but some will also be coming from the french fries because the deep-frying oil is largely made from animal fat. The total amount of animal fat in this meal, nearly 28 grams, is more than is recommended in any young person's diet *for a whole day.* For anyone trying to balance this meal, no saturated fats should be eaten in any other meal of the day, which is a very difficult task. The figure for sodium is also high; in fact, it approaches the levels that health experts recommend as a daily limit. Sodium is believed to increase the risk of high blood pressure.

The result is a meal with a high proportion of fat, too much salt, and a low level of nutrients for the calories provided. The reasons are simple: the fattiness of the hamburger meat, deep frying in animal fat, and the addition of salt in the burger, the bun, the sauces, and sprinkled on the fries. This particular example shows the general features of public relations material developed by several of the larger fast food companies. Material such as this can give an encouraging, scientific-looking image to food while ignoring uncomfortable facts that should also be given.

Task 1

Skim the text and decide whether the writer makes the following points about fast food meals. If he does, make a check mark [√] in the brackets.

[ ] The basic ingredients are bad for your health.
[ ] A fast food meal does not give you enough energy.
[ ] Fast food meals are worse for children than for adults.
[ ] Fast food is low in *all* minerals.
[ ] A fast food meal is low in Vitamin B_2.
[ ] Fast food meals contain too much saturated fat.

Adapted from Tim Lobstein, *Fast Food Facts* (London: Camden Press Ltd., 1988).

Task 2

How would you describe the content and attitude of this text?

a. informative and fair
b. merely stating the obvious
c. interesting facts, but too biased against fast food
d. trying to confuse us with tables and statistics

Task 3

Complete this crossword by using words from the text.

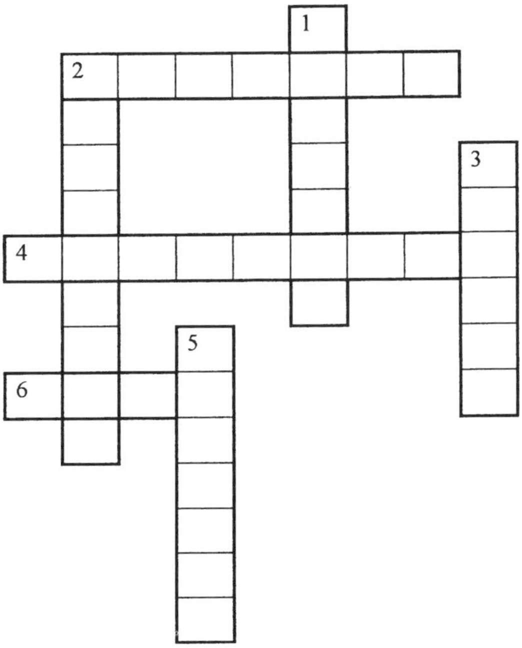

Down
1. Made less concentrated
2. Compensate (3 words)
3. Remove from our minds
5. How concentrated something is

Across
2. Make something difficult to understand
4. Vitamins and minerals that we need to keep us healthy
6. A measured amount

Task 4

What information does the writer tell us that the table from the fast food company does not? List four facts.

Task 5

Imagine that you eat the "typical meal combination" for lunch. What food would you eat for the rest of the day in order to achieve a balanced diet? Note your ideas below and then compare and discuss your answer in groups.

Breakfast	Lunch	Dinner
	large hamburger french fries apple pie regular cola	

Task 6

Discuss the following questions in groups.

a. Paragraph 2 says that fast food is usually "diluted" by adding extra "fat, sugar, or refined carbohydrates." Why would a fast food company want to do this?
b. Why do fast food companies print pamphlets like the table above, which show that their products are not very good for our health?
c. How could fast food companies' public relations material be more useful, or fairer, to the customer?

Fluency Activities

Sharing World Knowledge

Try to match the names of the dishes with their descriptions and their countries of origin. Then compare your ideas with the students sitting near you.

Haggis	rice dish with a meat and vegetable sauce, with nuts	Senegal, West Africa
Chelo khoresh	a mixture of taro, manioc, banana, and yam, with seafood, all wrapped in a palm leaf and cooked over charcoal	Mexico
Yassa	an egg custard made with coconut milk and baked inside a pumpkin	Thailand
Burrito	marinated, grilled chicken cooked in a pot with onions, garlic peppers, and lime juice, served with rice	Iran
Bougna	a sheep's stomach stuffed with the ground offal (liver, heart, kidneys, and intestines) of the animal	Melanesian Pacific Islands
Sankhaya	a soft corn pancake containing cooked meat and cheese	Scotland

If your group is of mixed ethnic origins, tell the other members about a favorite dish from your culture.

Stop and Think

Look at the meal in the picture. It looks delicious, doesn't it? Your teacher will tell you some facts about this food. After hearing each fact, fill in the appropriate information in the following table.

	Food Processes	Additives
The beef		
The mangoes		
The raspberry dessert		
The wine		
The vegetables		
The bread		

Analysis

Look at label *a*, and mark any ingredients you do not know.

a

CREAM OF MUSHROOM SOUP

INGREDIENTS: WATER, MUSHROOMS, VEGETABLE OIL, WHEAT FLOUR, CREAM, SALT, CORNSTARCH, WHEY, CALCIUM CASEINATE, MODIFIED FOOD STARCH, MONOSODIUM GLUTAMATE, SOY PROTEIN ISOLATE, NATURAL FLAVORING, YEAST EXTRACT, DEHYDRATED GARLIC.

How much cream does the soup contain?
How is the food starch "modified"?
Since the soup contains cream, mushrooms, and garlic, why is it necessary to add "natural flavoring"?
Can monosodium glutamate harm you?

Now look at label *b*. What question does it make you want to ask?

b

Dark Chocolate Cake Mix

INGREDIENTS

FLOUR, SUGAR, ANIMAL AND VEGATABLE FATS (CONTAINING EMULSIFIER 471), COCOA POWDER, BAKING POWDER, MALTODEXTRIN, WHEY POWDER, SOYA FLOUR, MODIFIED STARCH, SALT, COLORS E133 AND E155, FLAVOR.

Quiz

1. Which of these foods are high in fiber? Check [√] the correct answers.

[ ] brown bread
[ ] dried apricots
[ ] hard cheese
[ ] kidney beans
[ ] mackerel
[ ] sirloin steak
[ ] spinach

2. Why is fiber good for you? Check [√] the correct answers.

[ ] It helps people who are trying to lose weight.
[ ] It helps prevent constipation.
[ ] It helps strengthen your bones.
[ ] It increases your sex drive.
[ ] It is a good source of vitamins.
[ ] It may protect against bowel problems, including cancer.

3. Divide these foods according to whether they contain mainly saturated fats [S] or polyunsaturates [P].

[ ] bacon
[ ] chocolate
[ ] coconut oil
[ ] corn oil margarine
[ ] hazelnuts
[ ] soft cheese
[ ] trout

4.a. How many teaspoonsful of sugar are there in an average glass (200 ml) of cola? Check [√] the correct answer.

[ ] one
[ ] two
[ ] three
[ ] four
[ ] five

4.b. Look at this list of common processed foods and drinks. Check [√] those that you think contain no added sugar.

[ ] Hershey's chocolate
[ ] S&W canned red kidney beans
[ ] Hellman's real mayonnaise
[ ] Coleman's prepared English mustard
[ ] Heinz tomato ketchup
[ ] Schweppe's tonic water

5. Are the following statements true [T] or false [F]?

[ ] If you eat a balanced diet, you do not need to add salt to your food.
[ ] Sea-salt does not raise your blood pressure.
[ ] We need only 1 gram of salt a day.
[ ] After heavy exercise it is a good idea to take extra salt.

Answers: 1. Score 1 point each for dried apricots, spinach, kidney beans and brown bread; deduct 1 point if you marked any of the others. 2. Score 1 point each for losing weight, preventing constipation, and protecting against bowel problems; deduct 1 point if you marked any of the others. 3. Saturated fats: bacon, chocolate, coconut oil, soft cheese. Polyunsaturates: corn oil margarine, hazelnuts, trout. Score 1 point for each correct one. 4a. Five teaspoonsful. Score 1 point for correct answer. 4b. They all contain added sugar. Score one point for each unmarked box. 5. T, F, T, F. Score two points for every correct answer.

Rating

—above 24 points: Well done! Are you a nutritionist?
—18 to 23 points: You know a lot about healthy eating.
—11 to 17 points: You need to improve your knowledge about healthy eating.
—10 points or less: We hope nobody comes to you for advice about food!

Creative Cookery

Here is a list of ingredients. In pairs, make an interesting meal for two, using as many of them as you need.

rice	a small chicken	macaroni	shrimp
plain flour	two trout	green beans	lentils
six eggs	a piece of beefsteak		

potatoes	tomatoes	mushrooms	apples	eggplant
spinach	bell peppers	bananas	onions	almonds
garlic	spinach	coconut	strawberries	lemons

salt	milk	soy sauce	yogurt
olive oil	unsalted butter	cheese	vinegar
sugar	a selection of herbs, spices, and flavorings		

Present your meal, as a menu or a drawing, to your class.

Project

Note down everything you eat for a few days. Organize your list by grouping items together in whatever way you want. Bring your organized list to class and compare it with other people's lists.

Debate

Divide yourselves into two teams (For and Against) and brainstorm as many arguments as you can. Then either split up your arguments among the team and each side take turns presenting and defending your case, or pair off with a member of the opposing team and argue it out face to face. Argue either for or against the following statement.

Everyone should be encouraged to be a vegetarian.

Teacher's Notes and Answer Key

Organic Vegetables—Paying Extra for Chemical-Free Produce

Task 1. We think the best summary is c.

Task 2. Suitable questions are as follows.

How much more expensive is it to eat organic vegetables?
What happened to the soil when Paul Harlow was using chemicals?
What did he replace the chemicals with?
Why is it difficult to grow organic tomatoes?
Why do farmers need government subsidy during the conversion period?

Of course there are many other suitable questions.

Task 3. The carpenter doesn't mind paying more for organic vegetables. Harlow now uses no chemicals whatsoever. His children can play safely on the farm. Wilson still uses pesticides on certain vegetables. Pierce wants the government to help farmers go organic. Legislators are under pressure from big business interests.

Task 4. a. 1. environmental; 2. manure; 3. yield
b. 1. soil; 2. hazardous; 3. detrimental

Fast Food

Task 1. No, No, Yes, No, Yes, Yes

Task 2. We think the best answer is a, but a case could be made for c.

Task 3.

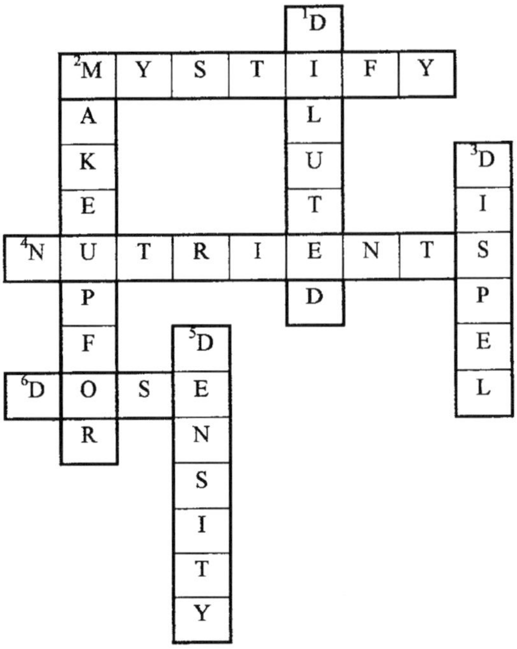

Task 4. The answers are in paragraphs 3 and 4. Suitable answers are: short in vitamin B_2, calcium, and iron; fat content is too high; saturated fat is especially high; too much sodium.

Fluency Activities

Sharing World Knowledge. Haggis: Scotland—a sheep's stomach stuffed with the ground offal (liver, heart, kidneys, and intestines) of the animal; *Chelo khoresh*: Iran—rice dish with a meat and vegetable sauce, with nuts; *Yassa*: Senegal, West Africa—marinated, grilled chicken cooked in a pot with onions, garlic peppers, and lime juice, served with rice; *Burrito*: Mexico—a soft corn pancake containing cooked meat and cheese; *Bougna*: Melanesian Pacific Islands—a mixture of taro, manioc, banana, and yam, with seafood, all wrapped in a palm leaf and cooked over charcoal; *Sankhaya*: Thailand—an egg custard made with coconut milk and baked inside a pumpkin.

Stop and think. Dictate the following, sentence by sentence.

The beef comes from a calf that had hormone injections to make it grow faster, and it was sprayed with sulphur dioxide to make it look fresh and red.

The mangoes were ripened artificially with nitrous oxide gas.

The raspberry dessert is made from artificial coloring, artificial flavoring, artificial preservatives, sugar, starch, and fat but contains no fruit.

The wine has sulphur dioxide added to preserve it.
The vegetables were irradiated to stop them from spoiling.
The white bread has been bleached and has added sugar and chemicals.

Analysis. The information on the label does not allow the reader to answer these perfectly reasonable questions. What does this tell us about the information provided by the manufacturer?

Quiz. Organize the students into groups of three and have one member of each group read each question aloud while the other two listen. All three then discuss it and agree on an answer, which is noted down. When they have finished the quiz, tell them to work out their scores by looking at the answer key. As feedback, discuss the results as a class.

Creative Cookery. Students should not be given too much guidance about how they organize their list of foods into groups. Most will probably group foods according to what they are: meat, vegetables, etc. Some may do it according to calories, fats, etc. A few may do it in other ways: foods they love, ones they like quite a lot, etc. The hope is that responses will be diverse!

Information from Eric Millstone, *Food Additives* (Harmondsworth: Penguin, 1986), 28, 50–51.

Unit 3
For Whose Benefit?

Guano and Fishmeal

Prereading

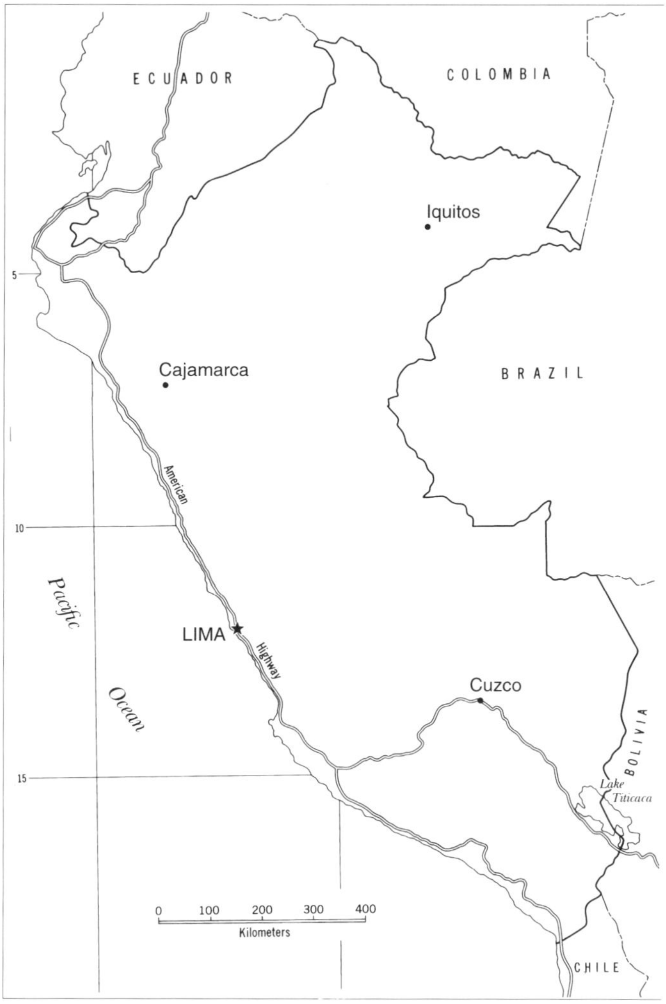

Which country is this? Do you know anything else about this country?

Reading

Look at task 1 below and then read through the text quickly, without using a dictionary.

First guano and now fishmeal: ironic that a country with stagnant agricultural production should have produced the richest natural fertilizers ever found. Guano (from Runasimi *wanu*, "dung") was also a product of the anchoveta—thick deposits of droppings from the host of seabirds who fed on them. In Inca times, these birds were protected, and the guano was mined at a rate calculated not to exceed its accumulation. Even so, thousands of tons were transported annually to the highlands, where the guano was used to shorten the growing season of maize and thus allow unprecedented yields from irrigated terracing. Systematic use of fertilizer was unknown at this time in Europe and the practice was soon forgotten in Peru after the Conquest. But in the nineteenth century science "discovered" fertilizer; mummified pelican droppings were again suddenly in demand.

What followed could well form the plot of a morality play devised to expose the effects of an unbridled free-market economy on weak countries and fragile environments. Exploitation of guano far exceeded deposition, and the human tragedy of the workers was shocking even by the barbarous standards of the day. Highland Runa died so fast on the acrid, arid islands that labor had to be found elsewhere. Chinese coolies were enticed by contracts that specifically excluded guano work, but they found themselves in chain gangs on the islands nonetheless. Many committed suicide (when they had the chance) by jumping into the sea. In one particularly savage episode, 720 Easter Island natives were brought to Peru; 620 died in the labor, and the remaining 100 took smallpox back to their island when they returned.

The resource became a government monopoly, but the concessions were operated mostly by British businessmen. An Englishman visiting Peru described his fellow countrymen as "gaining fortunes after such a fashion as only . . . a corrupt government could sanction or connive at." The money flooding into the Peruvian exchequer paid for a few flashy engineering projects—including Meiggs's Central Railway—and a military buildup that culminated in the War of the Pacific (1879–1883), in which Chile defeated Peru and Bolivia. Peru emerged totally bankrupt from the absurd conflict and was forced to sign over the entire guano operation to a consortium of foreign bankers.

Not long after the guano deposits were finally exhausted, the fishmeal process was discovered. From about 1950 Chimbote became the center of a similar onslaught on the anchoveta shoals. So many fish were "harvested" that the seabirds died in thousands from starvation. The perfidy of the Humboldt Current merely hastened the death of the coastal ecology.

It is easy to criticize the Peruvians for making the same mistake twice; but the real blame must lie with a dominant world civilization based on the short-sighted profit motive and the frightening myth of constant expansion. The plot of the guano story is perennial: in Bolivia during the same period a few tin barons got fabulously rich, thousands of Indian miners died, and Europe built up a canning industry at bargain rates; in Canada today, Indians and farmers are pushed off their land while oil companies make big profits feeding big cars with gasoline.

The Incas, who had no concept of progress, planned for eternity.

Task 1

Which of these statements is the best summary of the text?

a. The exploitation of guano and fishmeal has been of great importance to the Peruvian economy over the past 150 years.
b. The Incas were better at managing their natural resources than the modern Peruvian state.
c. The exploitation of Peru's guano and fishmeal is only one example of the economic domination of the Third World by the First.
d. Since the Peruvians did not understand the value of fertilizer, they used up the guano and fishmeal too quickly.

Task 2

Put these events into the order in which they happened by numbering them from [1] to [7].

[ ] Overfishing of anchoveta begins.
[ ] With the Spanish Conquest, the use of guano dies out.
[ ] Europeans start using guano as fertilizer.
[ ] The Incas use guano in a balanced way.
[ ] Both seabirds and anchoveta disappear.
[ ] Guano deposits are finished.
[ ] Discovery of process for using fish as fertilizer.

From Ronald Wright, *Cut Stones and Crossroads* (New York: Viking Penguin, 1984), 66–68.

Task 3

Look through the text and make two lists of words that are connected with (a) food production and (b) commerce. Then compare your lists with your partner.

Food Production	Commerce

Task 4

Look at the words and phrases in the following paragraphs of the text, and decide what they refer to.

Paragraph 1	at this time (when?)
	the practice (what practice?)
Paragraph 3	the resource (what resource?)
	the money (what money?)
Paragraph 5	the same mistake (what mistake?)
	during the same period (when?)

Task 5

Together with your partner, think of possible reasons why (a) the use of guano as fertilizer was forgotten after the Spanish Conquest and (b) the guano was so quickly exhausted after the business was sold to American bankers.

Task 6

Look at the last sentence of the text again.
Do you agree with the writer's opinion that the Incas used their natural resources more intelligently than modern business corporations? In groups, think of other ways in which modern societies fail to "plan for eternity."

Bangladesh's Penny Bank

Prereading

a. Look at the map and draw lines to separate the developed and underdeveloped parts of the world. Mark in Peru, which you've just read about, and Bangladesh, which is the subject of the next text.

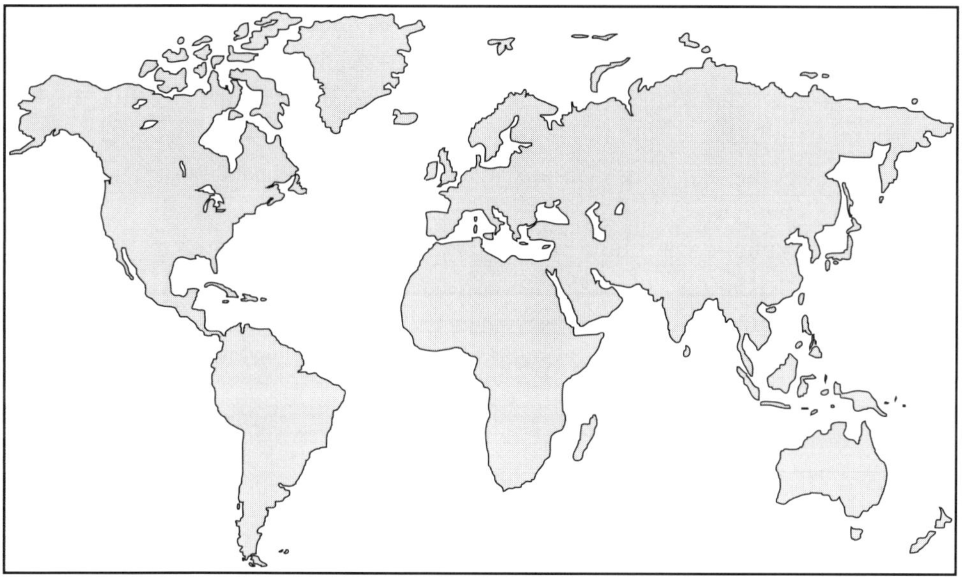

b. Which words associated with banking do you think will appear in the text?

Reading

Suruj Tangail is a village like thousands of others in Bangladesh, except that it boasts a school—not a common sight in Bangladesh—and a large blue concrete building that looks out of place in the paddy fields: it is a branch of the Grameen Bank, an establishment that specializes in mini-loans to the very poor. The school, in fact, is a project funded by the bank.

The Grameen Bank also helps people directly. In the next village, a mother of six worked for years, like many other women, polishing rice for a merchant. She used to slave away all day, getting only a bowl of rice and a little meat as wages. To begin working for herself and earn 25 takas (32 takas = 1U.S.$) a day, she needed an initial investment of 250 takas, a "large sum," in her words. She eventually raised the money from the bank. Now that she is no longer almost a slave, she is thinking of asking for another loan to buy a dairy cow.

The Grameen Bank was begun in 1969 by Muhammad Yunus, a young economics professor at the University of Chittagong. To disprove a common belief among bankers that it is impossible to make loans to the poor, he decided to give landless peasants the chance to buy income-generating equipment. The system works as follows: those applying for loans, all of them from very poor rural backgrounds, first have to form a group of five. To start with, only two of the five are entitled to a loan. The others in turn will obtain credit only if the initial borrowers repay both interest and capital over a period of 52 weeks. The group thus has a collective responsibility to ensure repayment: this means that collateral is unnecessary.

The loans are small—up to a maximum of 5,000 takas ($160) a year. All loans carry a 16 per cent interest rate. By the end of 1988 the bank had half a million customers and 500 branches and was paying out loans worth a total of about 80 million takas ($256,000) a month. The most striking fact about the bank is its quite amazing loan repayment rate of 98 per cent—"any banker's dream," says Yunus.

This contrasts with the record of the big international banks in Bangladesh. The *Los Angeles Times* estimated in 1987 that only 10 per cent of the 800 million U.S.$ loaned to Bangladesh by the World Bank and the Asian Development Bank had been repaid, and that middlemen had filled their own pockets as a result of government corruption.

The Grameen Bank's success comes not only from its several thousand employees (it has never used foreign consultants) but also from women. As Yunus explains: "Almost 80 per cent of our borrowers are women. Why, you may ask? Because women experience poverty and hunger much more intensively than men. Traditionally they are expected to look after the house and feed the children with almost no money at all. They are the ones who experience the worst pain when their children go hungry or fall ill. Give women like that a chance to fight hunger and poverty, and you'll find they're braver than their menfolk."

Yunus says there are prejudices against granting loans to the poor: "It's a question of attitudes, ideology, and, above all, ignorance of the facts among those in charge of aid policies. For 40 years they've been lending to governments, elites, and those in charge of major projects. The result is that poverty has not decreased and the debt burden has increased. On the other hand, when people are allowed to manage their own development, the results are remarkable and the repayment rate is unbelievably good."

Task 1

Match these paragraph summaries to the seven paragraphs in the text.

[ ] the record of the big banks
[ ] a case study
[ ] successful and unsuccessful development
[ ] the size of the Grameen Bank
[ ] a village with a difference
[ ] the importance of women
[ ] how the Grameen Bank works

Task 2

What are the differences between the Grameen Bank and the big international banks? Try to find at least four differences (compare, for example, the size of loans, the repayment rate, who borrows the money?) and note them below.

Grameen Bank	International Banks
1.	
2.	
3.	
4.	

Adapted from an article by Roland-Pierre Paringaux, "Bangladesh's Penny Bank Gives Hope to the Rural Poor," in the *Guardian Weekly*, *Le Monde* section, 30 April 1989, 15–16.

Task 3

Organize these words from the text into two or more groups, and explain why you grouped the words in that way.

village	rural	school	paddy field
cow	middlemen	merchant	elites
development	poverty	consultants	rice
professor	government	peasant	banker

Task 4

Why does Yunus believe that aid policies have failed? List the reasons he gives for the failure of such policies, and any other reasons you can find in the text. Then add any further reasons you can think of.

Yunus's reasons
Other reasons from the text
Your own ideas

Task 5

What other questions would you like to ask Yunus? Think of at least three, and compare them with the students sitting next to you.

Fluency Activities

Brainstorm

Make two lists by writing down the names of the following.

six countries that are developed
six countries that are underdeveloped

Do this quickly—write down the names you first think of.

Developed Countries	Undeveloped Countries

What criteria did you use for judging whether a country is developed or not? Write down your criteria here.

Evaluation

Look at the following criteria and decide which you expect to be high in underdeveloped countries and which you expect to be low.

a. population growth
b. life expectancy
c. infant deaths
d. workforce in agriculture
e. urban population
f. literacy
g. telephones in use
h. children at school
i. income per person
j. human rights
k. patients per doctor
l. calories per person

High	Low

Now look at the following table and analyze the data to rank the seven countries (New Zealand, Ireland, Saudi Arabia, China, Botswana, Brazil, and Jamaica) from most to least developed.

	New Zealand	Ireland	Saudi Arabia	China	Botswana	Brazil	Jamaica
Population growth	0.9%	–0.1%	4.2%	1.2%	3.5%	2.4%	1.1%
Life expectancy	74.9	74.3	63.5	68.4	58.2	66.6	75.8
Infant deaths (per 1,000 births)	11	9	85	44	67	63	20
Workforce in agriculture f&f[a]	11%	14.5%	8.4%	63%	54%	30%	33%
Urban population	84%	56%	66%	21%	16%	68%	48%
Literacy	100%	100%	46%	72%	71%	79%	89%
Telephones: people per phone	1.5	3.8	8.4	166	55	12	18
Children at high school	85%	96%	42%	39%	29%	35%	58%
Murder rate (per 100,000 people)	3	0.5	1	1	11	—	18
GDP[b] per person (U.S.$)	11,544	9,181	5,311	301	1,488	2,451	1,298
Civil rights rating[c]	1.0	1.6	6.0	6.7	3.1	4.7	2.4
Patients per doctor	417	830	1,202	737	6,748	1,200	6,400
Daily calories per person	3,573	3,699	2,940	2,426	2,352	2,578	2,544

[a] f&f = forestry and fishing.

[b] GDP = gross domestic product (the value of everything made in the country).

[c] Civil rights rated on a scale of 1 (best record) to 7 (worst record) worldwide.

Compare your rankings with other students and explain any differences in your rankings. Was there anything in the table that made the ranking difficult?

Stop and Think

What do you know about the following: U.N. aid agencies, the International Monetary Fund (I.M.F.), the World Bank? What kind of work do they do? Read the following facts about official aid and development.

Samples of UNESCO Expenditures in 1984	U.S.$
Education of handicapped African children	$49,000
Curriculum development in Pakistan	$7,200
Teacher training in Honduras	$1,000
President's and executives' travel and lodging	$1,759,548

President Mobutu of Zaire, the eighth poorest country in the world, has reportedly helped himself to 20% of all foreign aid to Zaire since he seized power in 1965. He has bought 51 Mercedes cars, 11 castles, and mansions, hotels, luxury apartments in Europe, Australia and the United States but dismissed 7,000 teachers for "budgetary reasons" in the mid-eighties.

In May 1990, Britain's aid Minister boasted that Britain gets orders worth U.S.$1.75 for every $1.00 it puts into aid agencies like the United Nations, the World Bank, and the IMF. Between 1983 and 1985, in ten Latin American countries with big debt problems, moneyed people deposited U.S.$44.2 billion in Western banks.

Philippines: results of 1984 IMF 'adjustment' policy:	
GNP	fell to 1975 level
Workers' earnings	fell 31–48% from 1982 levels
Education spending	fell to 30% less than in 1979

Between 1982 and 1987 British banks received over U.S.$125 billion in debt-service payments from Latin America. This is equal to every Latin American person paying U.S.$64 a year to the banks. During the same period, direct British aid to Latin America was under 13 cents per person per year.

Which of these facts surprises you most? What questions about development and aid do they make you want to ask? Using the facts given here and your knowledge of the world, can you construct an explanation of the purpose(s) behind rich countries' development aid?

Interpretation

Look at the following graph. What does it tell us about world money flow?

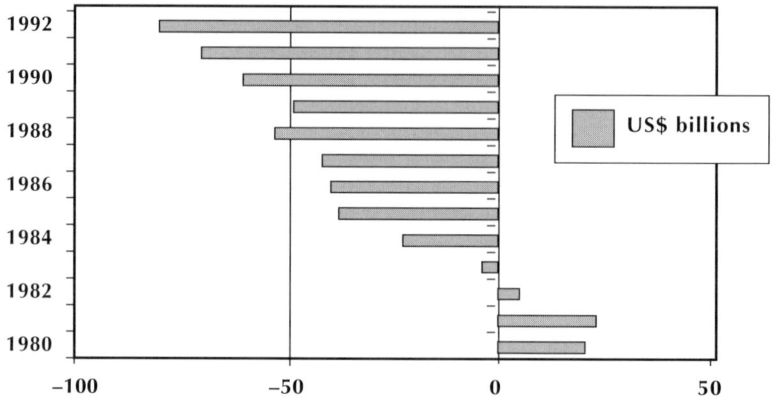

Financial flows from poor to rich countries (1980–92)

Can you guess what this money flow consists of? Note down your ideas and compare them.

Which of these items flows mainly

from rich to poor countries?
from poor to rich countries?

Can you explain why money is flowing increasingly from poor countries to rich ones?

From Ben Jackson, World Development Movement, *Poverty and the Planet* (Harmondsworth: Penguin, 1990), 96; and Guy Arnold, *The End of the Third World* (New York: St. Martin's Press, 1993), 89. Data derived from World Bank statistics.

Project

Choose a country in which you are interested and collect information about it. Present this information to your classmates as a poster. The sort of information you present should let your classmates judge the "level of development" of the country you have chosen. What criteria did you use to demonstrate this?

The Trading Game

You are now ready to play the trading game. Follow your teacher's instructions.

Now discuss what happened during the game. The following questions may help you.

What did you find frustrating/unfair about the game?
Did other groups cooperate or help?
How did the "economic" changes affect you?
Did you make any alliances or deals with other groups?
In what ways does this game reflect the real world of international trade? What do your paper, pencils, etc., represent?
Which countries are in a similar position to your group? to the other groups?

Teacher's Notes and Answer Key

Guano and Fishmeal

Prereading. The country is Peru. Lima is its capital city. Cuzco was the ancient capital of the Inca empire in the Andes mountains. In 1995 a Peruvian of Japanese descent, Alberto Fujimori, was reelected president. The Inca was the name of the rulers of an Andean empire that included the modern states of Colombia, Peru, and northern Chile. Generations of Inca ruled this empire before the arrival of the Spanish conquerors in the sixteenth century, who destroyed it completely in their search for gold.

Task 1. c is the best summary.

Task 2. 6, 2, 3, 1, 7, 4, 5

Task 3. food production: agricultural, fertilizers, guano, yield, maize, growing season, irrigated, terracing, fishmeal process, harvested, canning industry; *commerce*: resource, contracts, businesspeople, bankrupted, bankers, profit motive, expansion, bargain rates, calculated, accumulation, free-market economy, yield, monopoly, consortium, concessions

Task 4. at this time: in Inca times (before the sixteenth century); *the practice*: systematic use of fertilizers; *the resource*: guano; *the money*: from selling guano mining contracts; *the same mistake*: exhausting natural resources; *during the same period*: the nineteenth century.

Task 5. This is an open-ended question. Possible reasons include (a) the Spanish conquistadores did not think that the Inca "savages" could teach them anything; the Incas were unwilling to tell their secrets to the Spanish conquerors and colonizers; the Inca were dispossessed from the land by Spanish settlers, so their agricultural knowledge was lost; (b) the U.S. bankers were interested in making as much money as quickly as possible (true venture capitalists); there was no philosophy of environmental conservation at that time; people believed that technological progress could solve everything, so that once the guano was exhausted a new fertilizer would be discovered.

Task 6. Again these are open-ended questions. The reading text suggests that the Incas did use natural resources more intelligently. They understood that it is environmentally (and economically?) unsound to use up natural resources more quickly than they can be replaced. Other examples of this short-sighted lack of planning are deforestation, waste of energy resources, and throw-away goods like plastic bags.

Bangladesh's Penny Bank

Task 1. 5, 2, 7, 4, 1, 6, 3

Task 2. the size of loans: small—up to 5,000 takas a year, compared to giant international loans for large projects; *the repayment rate*: 98% for the Grameen Bank, 10% for international loans; *who borrows*: almost 80% are women at the Grameen Bank, the government, elites, and major project controllers from international banks; *results of loans*: people can manage their own development with the Grameen Bank, but with international banks, Bangladesh's debt burden has increased with no decrease in poverty.

Task 3. There are many different possible criteria for grouping the words, for example: town, country, and state; people's occupations, places, and institutions; food production, education, business, and government.

Task 4. Yunus's reasons: the people in charge of aid policies are ignorant of the situation in Bangladesh, are prejudiced against granting loans to the poor, who are actually the ones best placed to fight against poverty; *other reasons from the text*: corruption in the government, which allows loans to go to middlemen who are not obliged to repay the loans; *other possible reasons*: the belief that collateral is essential for loan repayment, so landless peasants are a "worse risk" than government; international bankers are overwhelmingly male and will only lend to other men. Can you think of others?

Task 5. This is an open-ended question. I would want to ask him what role he thinks international banks could play, why he never uses foreign consultants, and how many Grameen Bank employees are women.

Fluency Activities

Brainstorm. The countries of western Europe, North America, and Japan are considered developed. Other East Asian countries such as Korea, Taiwan, Hong Kong, and Singapore are often called "newly industrialized." The former Soviet-bloc countries are difficult to classify—industrialized but underdeveloped? The rest of the world is therefore considered to be in various stages of development. This should raise some doubts in your mind about the meaning (or lack of it) of "(under)development." The criteria by which "development" can be measured are listed in the Evaluation section of the text.

Evaluation. The average person would probably expect population growth, infant deaths, and the agricultural workforce to be high and all the rest to be low, given the stereotypical view of an underdeveloped country. We hope that the statistics presented in the table will go some way toward exploding this stereotype. Obviously, there is no "correct" ranking, though most will have put New Zealand or Ireland first. The information in the table comes from *Vital World Statistics*, (London: Economist, 1990) and G. T. Kurian, *The New Book of World Rankings* (London: Facts on File, 1991).

Stop and Think. Again, the purpose of the exercise is to help students question conventional ideas about the "goodness" of "development." We hope that by this stage they will have realized that a great deal of development aid (most of which comes from ordinary taxpayers like the students and their families) at best fails to reach the poor and at worst helps to make their lives even more miserable. Is the real purpose of development aid to ensure markets for the products of the industrialized countries? The information in the boxes comes from Graham Hancock, *Lords of Poverty* (London: Macmillan Ltd., 1989), 62–64, 90, 178, 182, 189; and Ben Jackson, *Poverty and the Planet* (London: Penguin, 1990), 136.

Interpretation. Did students mention the following items: debt service, aid, loans, trade (commodities, manufactured goods, services)? Obviously debt service moves from poor to rich, as do commodities (usually natural resources like timber and coffee). The rest moves from rich to poor, which again suggests that the real purpose of development aid and loans is to benefit the rich.

Project. Students should be applying what they have learned in this unit to the information they gather about the country they have chosen. Rather than just collecting descriptive information of the tourist guide variety about a country, students should be encouraged to look at statistics and other information that tell us something about the country's quality of life. Again it is hoped that students will choose different criteria for judging "quality of life," thus sparking discussion in class when students make their presentations to classmates.

The Trading Game

Time and Space

An hour for the game plus discussion
5 or 6 groups of 3–6 players each

Equipment (for 30 players)

1 sheet of plain paper per player
1 "$100 bill" per player
2 sheets of colored sticky paper—4 × 4 inches.
4 pairs of scissors
4 rulers
2 compasses for drawing circles
2 set squares
2 protractors
14 lead pencils
extra pencils and paper for emergencies

Setting up the Game

Divide students into groups (A, B, C, plus A1, B1, C1 if needed), allocating each group an area in the classroom.

Allocate resource packs as follows.

Group A (A1): 10 sheets of paper, 2 pencils, $300
Group B (B1): 4 sheets of paper, 2 pencils, 1 ruler, 1 sheet of colored sticky paper, $400
Group C (C1): 1 sheet of paper, 3 pencils, 1 ruler, 1 compass, 1 protractor, 1 set square, $800

Draw the following shapes and their values on the board.

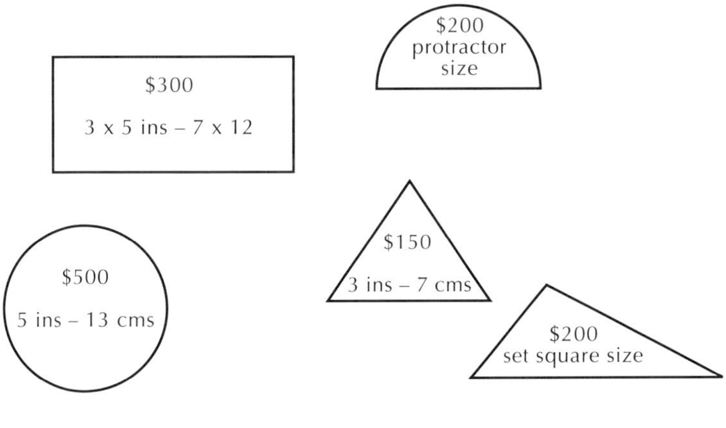

Rules for Playing the Game

Teacher's role is to be banker and leader. As banker you keep an account for each group.
Each group makes as much money as possible using only the materials given.
Money is made by producing paper shapes and giving them to the banker (teacher), who credits the group's account with the value of the shape.
All shapes MUST be cut using scissors and must be exactly the size shown on the board.
Any disagreements are settled by the leader (teacher).

Playing the Game

Groups begin manufacturing paper shapes, if they can.
At the beginning, players will probably have many questions. (Can we borrow scissors? Can we trade? Why haven't we got scissors? What's the sticky paper for?) Resist all temptation to answer these questions—just repeat the rules or stay silent. All initiative for trading should come from the students.
After a while, make some of the following changes, which approximate economic changes in the real world.

change the values of some of the shapes
give a new supply of raw material (i.e., paper) to one group
discreetly tell one or two groups that if they attach a square centimeter of sticky paper to their shapes, they will get four times the value for them
offer aid to a group (e.g., a short-term loan of scissors) on certain terms (e.g., three shapes per minute of the loan must be repaid to the banker as interest)

Allow manufacturing and trading to continue for about 30 minutes. Stop the game and tell groups how much they have in their accounts.

Follow-up Discussion (whole class)

Get groups to recall what happened during the game and to draw parallels between elements in the game and the real world of international trade, such as the following.

the paper = raw materials
the rest of the equipment = technology
the sticky paper = a resource whose true value is not fully understood by everyone
changing the value of the shapes = changing market values because of over supply, outdated technology, etc.

Examples of countries that are in similar positions to groups A, B, and C are: A, Kenya, Burma; B, India, Peru; C, United States, Japan.

Thanks to Christian Aid, P.O. Box 100, London SE1 7RT, England, for permission to use the Trading Game.

Unit 4
Glad to Be Gay?

High School Prom

Prereading

The following words all appear in the text. Check the meanings of any that you don't know. Then decide which of them are positive words and which are negative and put them in two lists.

honesty	gay	discrimination	selfish
be left out	dignity	rights	violently
happiness	prejudice	homosexuality	a lie

Positive Words	Negative Words

Reading

This text is from the autobiography of Aaron, a nineteen-year old. It tells us how he makes a decision that dramatically affects his life.

Look at Task 1 below and then read through the text quickly, without using a dictionary.

Everyone was talking about the prom after Mr. Lynch's speech. The girls planned to make or buy their gowns. Some guys chatted about last year's prom. But, like always, I was left out of these discussions. Through all of my high school years I had been left out, and I was tired of it. I wanted to be part of the group like all the other students.

The simple, obvious thing would have been to go to the senior prom with a girl. But that would have been a lie—a lie to myself, to the girl, and to all the other students. What I wanted to do was to take a male date. But as my friend Paul had shown the year before, such honesty is not always easy.

There was an important difference between Paul's case and mine, though. Paul had not been able to fight for his rights because he was seventeen at the time. I was now eighteen and legally able to make my own decisions. If I wanted to go to the prom with a male escort and the school tried to stop me, I could take the case to court.

But should I do that? This would require much thought if I was to make a decision without being selfish, uncaring, or irrational. If I went to the prom with another guy, what would be the benefits? For myself, it would mean participating in an important social event and doing so with a clear conscience and a sense of honesty. But how would it affect the rest of the people involved?

I believed that those who had themselves faced discrimination or prejudice would immediately understand what I was doing. There would be others who may never have had direct experiences with prejudice but would recognize my right to the date of my choice. These people may have been misled to believe that homosexuality is wrong, but they could still understand that my rights were being denied.

At the other extreme were the homophobes, who might react violently. But the example I set would be perfect for everyone. We would be just one more happy couple. Our happiness together would be something kids could understand. I would be showing that my dignity and value as a human being were not affected by my sexual preference. I concluded that taking a guy to the prom would be a strong, positive statement about the existence of gay people. Any opposition to my case (and I expected quite a lot) would show the negative side of society—not of homosexuality.

Adapted from Aaron Fricke, *Reflections of a Rock Lobster* (Boston: Alyson Publications, 1985), 69–70.

Task 1

Which paragraph tells you about the following?

[ ] his legal position
[ ] the difficulties of making the decision
[ ] what he hopes to show by going to the prom
[ ] why he wanted to go to the prom
[ ] the people who would sympathize with him
[ ] who he really wants to take to the prom.

Task 2

Find words or phrases in the text which mean the same as

someone who accompanies you to a dance/party (para. 3)
without thinking carefully and clearly (para. 4)
the feeling that you are acting fairly and honestly (para. 4)
people who fear and hate homosexuals (para. 6)
whether you are attracted to men or to women (para. 6)

Task 3

In paragraphs 2 and 3 Aaron talks about Paul and about "taking the case to court." In pairs, try to find suitable answers to the following questions.

a. What had Paul wanted to do? Why had he failed?

____

____

____

____

b. What does Aaron want to do? What "case" can he take to court?

____

____

____

____

c. Is he likely to win such a case in the United States? Why (not)?

Task 4

Which of these words describe Aaron's character? Choose as many words as you want.

mature	crazy	bitter	effeminate	selfish
brave	passionate	vain	short-sighted	unrealistic
sensitive	gentle	indiscreet	sociable	confident

Add any other words that you think describe him.

Task 5

In Aaron's opinion, what are the advantages and disadvantages of taking a male date to the dance? List them in the following chart.

Advantages	Disadvantages

Can you think of any others?

Task 6

What do you think happened?
Did Aaron decide to take a guy to the prom? Who? What did the school do? Did the case go to court? How did the matter end?

Fear of the "Naturals"

Prereading

Homosexuality is legal in some places, illegal in others; in some places gay men and lesbians have the same legal rights as the rest of the population, in others they do not. Look at the list of countries below and use your knowledge of the world to place them on a line according to what you imagine the legal status of homosexual people to be in those countries.

Denmark	England	Thailand	Singapore	New Zealand
Ghana	Egypt	Brazil	Chile	Sri Lanka

100% equal rights	illegal and criminal

Reading

The following report was published in 1990, a few months before the end of the Soviet Union.

Look at Task 1 below and then read through the text quickly, without using a dictionary.

Roman Kalinin recently returned to Moscow after a month in California as a guest of U.S. gay activists. The visit was a **revelation.**

"Since coming back here, I've stopped trying to save myself. I just want to help the next generation of Soviet gays to be happier than we were," he says. Grave words for a 24-year-old, but Kalinin has reason to be gloomy. Last year he set up an underground gay newspaper called *Tema* or "theme," one of the **code words** for homosexuality, and also cofounded a tiny Union for Sexual Minorities. Since then he has been **hounded** from his flat and warned by the **militia** that he will face **prosecution** for a yet to be specified crime.

Homosexuality is illegal in the Soviet Union under Article 121 of the criminal code. The article was introduced in 1933, and in 1934 Maxim Gorky articulated the official attitude, writing in *Pravda*: "**Eliminate** homosexuality and you will make fascism disappear." The law was applied assiduously. A woman who recently tried to register a gay community center with the democrat-dominated Leningrad City was promptly arrested for trying to legitimize a "criminal" organisation. Gay **activists** estimate that 25,000 men are in prison "under the Article" with 800 prosecutions in 1989 alone.

Even in the most liberal Russian circles homosexuality is regarded as an unfortunate **affliction** better ignored, while the official artistic community displays the same open **ambivalence** to gays as it does to Jews. "The very concept of gay rights is completely unknown here," says one gay man who is active in unofficial circles. "Most Russian gay men just want to be **decriminalized.** We don't define ourselves politically by our sexuality, like gay men in the West. Yet no one supports us; even liberals seem to think that until naturals (straight people) have the right to choose their president, then blues (gay men) should stop making demands."

"The main intention of *Tema* is to help gay brothers and sisters find each other," says Kalinin. Although each edition of the thrice-yearly paper has sold 10,000 copies, the gay population is completely **dispersed.** "The KGB only need to arrest one percent of gay men to terrify everyone. Many people have to work as KGB informers to avoid prison," he says.

Many people genuinely believe that homosexuality started in the labor camps during the 1930s and is just another "punishment" inflicted on the unfortunate Russians by Communism. Others blame pesticides and flatly refuse to believe that lesbianism even exists.

Prudishness can work in favor of gay men, as one gay activist explained. "My friends have been lovers for five years and regularly share a bed at their parents' house without anyone suspecting anything or asking any awkward questions." However, when Russian parents do get suspicious it is not unknown for them to haul their children off to the local hospital. There they may be unfortunate enough to come under the care of a psychiatrist who still believes in the concept of "sluggish schizophrenia," said to lead to "parasitic behaviour," but to be treatable by heavy doses of drugs and "**corrective therapy.**"

At the Bechtev Research Institute in St. Petersburg, psychotherapist Dmitri Asaev specializes in homosexuality. "Many men end up here after suicide attempts. I try to help them to come to terms with their condition, to form stable relationships and learn how to live in a homophobic society. . . . We have all absorbed the brutalizing effect of **totalitarianism,** which refuses to tolerate any form of **dissidence** in the private sphere."

Asaev is hopeful that AIDS will force a change in the law and that a Russian gay community will emerge—lawyers within the Ministry of Health have been arguing for over a year about whether Article 121 should be dropped from the new criminal code. Meanwhile most Russian gays are staying in the relative safety of the **closet,** while activists are relying on the Soviet government's concern with international opinion to protect them.

Adapted from an article by Paulette Farsides in the *Guardian*, 11 January 1990, 24.

In 1991 Roman Kalinin decided to stand against Boris Yeltsin as a gay candidate for the presidency of Russia. He now runs Moscow's first gay discotheque. The Russian Duma, or Parliament, repealed Article 121 of the criminal code and in 1993 set the age of consent (the age at which people are legally entitled to have sex or get married) at age 18 for everyone, regardless of sexual orientation. This is legally a better situation than that prevailing in Britain, which in 1996 still had differing ages of consent. There is still a great deal of harassment of and discrimination against gay people, particularly lesbians. The enforced hospitalization of Russian lesbians was cited as a cause for concern in the 1995 U.S. State Department report on human rights.

Task 1

Which of these is the best summary of the text?

a. Roman Kalinin's visit to California made him depressed about the gloomy situation of gays in his own country; however, there is some hope of changes for the better in the future.
b. Gay people in Russia have finally begun fighting against the unjust laws, official harassment, and social intolerance that they face in their daily lives.
c. Strict application of antihomosexual laws and rigid social intolerance make it difficult for Russian gays to lead normal lives and impossible for them to organize themselves politically.

Task 2

Are these statements true [T] or false [F]?

[ ] Because homosexuality is still considered a psychiatric disease, it is not uncommon for Russian gays to try to commit suicide.
[ ] The KGB arrested very many people for being homosexual and so gays were afraid to meet each other.
[ ] Becoming an activist for gay rights in Russia will immediately lead to police harassment.
[ ] Sexual prudishness and ignorance are very common in Russia.
[ ] Communists believe homosexuality was linked to fascism, while many Russian citizens believe it was a product of communism.

Task 3

Look at the words in **bold** in the text. Circle the ones that you don't know. Which of the words that you do not know prevent you from understanding something important in the text? Find out what they mean, preferably without using a dictionary.

Task 4

What does the text say about the following?

Homosexuals and the law
Police and KGB attitudes toward gays
The medical profession's attitudes
Artists' attitudes
Parents of gay people
Gay people's attitudes toward themselves

Task 5

List the various causes of homosexuality mentioned in the text.

Now use your own knowledge to list the causes of heterosexuality.

Fluency Activities

Opinion Survey

Check [√] the sentences that you agree with; rewrite the others to reflect your opinion.

[ ] Sexual relations between two men or two women are unnatural.

[ ] Nobody can control who they find attractive or who they fall in love with.

[ ] It is easy to recognize homosexuals by their clothes and gestures.

[ ] Everyone experiences homosexual feelings at some time in their life.

[ ] Certain professions, such as teaching and youth work, should not be open to homosexuals.

[ ] Schools should teach pupils about homosexuality positively.

[ ] Everyone knows someone who is homosexual.

In small groups, compare your answers, explaining any differences of opinion.

Reactions

Imagine that a close friend has just told you she/he is homosexual. What questions would you like to ask her/him? Note down your ideas and compare them with your partner.

Brainstorm

Your best friend has told you she/he is gay, but nobody else knows. What difficulties (things she/he can't say or do) will she/he experience? Think about the following areas, discuss in small groups, and list the difficulties.

At Work	Family Life	Going out on a Date

Information Sharing

What do you know about gay life in your hometown?

Are there any well-known gay people?
Are there any gay activist groups?
Are there places where gay people can meet?
Are gay people "in the closet" or can they be relatively open?

Commenting

Read the following quotations and say what you think about them.

a. "Those who behave in a homosexual fashion shall not enter the kingdom of God." (Pope John Paul II, 1986)
b. "If homosexuality were normal, God would have created Adam and Bruce." (Anita Bryant, entertainer)
c. "If God dislikes gays so much, how come He picked Michelangelo, a known homosexual, to paint the Sistine Chapel ceiling, while assigning Anita Bryant to go on TV and push orange juice?" (Mike Royko, columnist)
d. "I think extreme heterosexuality is a perversion." (Margaret Mead, anthropologist)
e. "Young people have the right to be brought up to understand that they may experience homosexual or heterosexual feelings or both, and that . . . both are to be welcomed as having potential to enrich their lives." (U.K. Green Party Manifesto)
f. "Remember, since homosexuals cannot have children of their own, the only way for them to expand their ranks is to recruit your children and mine." (The Reverend Jerry Falwell)
g. "You will never be rid of us because we produce ourselves out of your bodies." (Martha Shelley, writer)
h. "There is no need for parents to fear homosexual teachers. Ninety-seven percent of child seduction is heterosexual." (Dr. Benjamin Spock, professor of child development)
i. "2-4-6-8, gay is twice as good as straight." (1970s Gay Liberation Front chant)

Project

Look through recent newspapers and magazines and collect articles, stories, advertisements, etc., that feature gay people or homosexuality. Which give positive images, which are negative, and which are neutral?

Debate

Divide yourselves into two teams (For and Against) and brainstorm as many arguments as you can. Then either split up your arguments among the team and each side take turns presenting and defending your case, or pair off with a member of the opposing team and argue it out face to face. Argue either for or against the following statement.

Gay people have the right to equality before the law.

Teacher's Notes and Answer Key

High School Prom

Prereading. Honesty, dignity, and happiness are obviously positive words; selfish, prejudice, discrimination, be left out, violently, and a lie are negative. Which list did the class put gay, rights, and homosexuality in?

Task 1. 3, 4, 6, 1, 5, 2

Task 2. escort; irrational; clear conscience; homophobes; sexual preference

Task 3. Paul wanted to take a boy to the prom but failed because he was underage. Aaron wants to take a boy to the prom too. He can sue the school if they stop him, because he's 18. He is likely to win the case because it would be an infringement of his civil rights.

Task 5. Advantages: he wouldn't feel left out of the group; participating in an important social event; having a clear conscience and sense of honesty; setting an example; making a strong positive statement about the existence of gay people. *Disadvantages:* getting involved in a court case; it might have a bad effect on the rest of the people involved; violence from homophobes.
Note. It would be useful to ask students whom he means by "the rest of the people involved."

Task 6. Aaron decided to take Paul to the prom, and the school tried to stop him. Aaron therefore sued the school. The case did in fact go to court, and Aaron did win the right to take a male date to his high school prom.

Fear of the "Naturals"

Prereading. Denmark would be at the full equality end of the line, closely followed by New Zealand. The countries at the other extreme would be Singapore, Sri Lanka, and Chile; in all these countries homosexuality is a criminal offense. The other countries would be in the middle, though it is difficult to rank them: there may not be laws criminalizing homosexuality, but that does not mean there is legal equality. In England, for example, the age of consent (the age at which people may first have sex) was 18 for gay people and 16 for everyone else in 1996. Also, the culture of a society is very important: even if homosexuality is not forbidden, there may be strong religious or social attitudes against it. Thailand, for example, is quite tolerant, but Egypt and Brazil have religious taboos that influence people's attitudes toward sexuality. The following is a suggested answer to the question based on how much the law in each country protects or punishes gay people: Denmark, New Zealand, Thailand, Ghana, Brazil, Egypt, England, Chile, Singapore, Sri Lanka.

Task 1. c is the best summary.

Task 2. T, F, T, T, T

Task 3. Obviously everybody's answers will be different.

Task 4. The law: homosexuality is illegal according to article 121 of the Criminal Code introduced in 1933 (by Stalin!). *Police and KGB:* they harass activists (e.g., Kalinin and the woman in Leningrad City [St. Petersburg]); 25,000 gay men in prison; 800 prosecutions in 1989; many have to work as KGB informers to avoid prison. *Medical profession:* ranges from psychiatrists who think homosexuality is a disease (sluggish schizophrenia) treatable by drugs and corrective therapy to those like Asaev, who help gays come to terms with living in a homophobic society. *Artists:* have an ambivalent attitude. *Parents:* ranges from ignorance of their children's gayness to the belief that it is a disease. *Gay people:* a small number of activists, but most Russian gays stay in the closet and just want to be decriminalized.

Task 5. Causes of homosexuality: labour camps (in the 1930s), punishment inflicted by Communism, pesticides, mental disease, possibly fascism. *Causes of heterosexuality:* nobody would even think to ask this question! What does this tell us about the "causes" of homosexuality?

Fluency Activities

Opinion Survey. Please be careful not to let your own opinions influence or inhibit the students, particularly in the feedback stage. The third statement is definitely incorrect (at least in highly westernized cultures), while the last statement is almost certainly true (though many people will not know that they know someone who is gay). The other statements are, of course, all matters of opinion.

*Reactions.*This is an open-ended activity. Many people would want to ask questions such as: How long have you known you were gay? How do you meet other gay people? Who else knows you are gay? How did they react to the news? What was it like pretending to be heterosexual?

Brainstorm. This is an open-ended activity. Did students note the following suggestions? *At work:* always pretending to be heterosexual; listening to anti-gay jokes and remarks; telling lies or avoiding questions about relationships; not being able to get promoted because you are not married. *Family life:* pressure to get married and have children; not being able to talk to parents and relatives about your relationships/lover or your lifestyle; not enjoying the legal rights of married couples. *Going out on a date:* not being able to hold hands or kiss in public; not dancing together; not being given the "romantic" tables in restaurants.

Information sharing. This is a completely open-ended activity.

Commenting. This material can be exploited in many ways: you could ask students to identify which are pro-gay, which are anti-gay, and which take a neutral position; or to identify which contain facts and what the facts are; or which, if any, students agree with and why and which they disagree with and why. Some answers: *pro-gay*: i, possibly c, d, and g; *anti-gay*: a, b, f; *neutral*: e, h, possibly c and d. *Facts*: c, Michelangelo did paint the Sistine chapel, Anita Bryant did advertise orange juice; g, everyone (gay or straight) has a mother and a father; h, 97% of child seduction is heterosexual.

Project. Since it may be difficult to find positive images in countries where homosexuality is both illegal and not tolerated, teachers might try to supplement the articles that students gather with more positive images from North America, Australasia, or other countries where there is greater freedom of information about sexual orientation.

Unit 5
The Dream Sellers

The Want Makers

Prereading

Which of these brand names are famous where you come from? Please check (√) your answers. What sorts of products are they? Do you know the countries of origin of the companies that make these products?

	Famous	Description of Product	Country of Origin
Colgate			
American Express			
Chivas Regal			
Canon			
Pepsi			
Heineken			
Kodak			
Marlboro			
Nescafe			
Mercedes			
Lego			
McDonald's			
Levis			
KitKat			
Sony Walkman			
Kellogg's			
Lux			
Reebok			
Contac			

Reading

Look at task 1 below and then read through the text quickly, without using a dictionary.

Although vast numbers of companies advertise, just a few industries and some individual corporations dominate, often across the world. A breakdown of the top 100 advertisers in the United States in 1985 shows that 10 groups spent over $1 billion: the automobile industry, food, alcohol, candy and soft drinks, drugs and remedies, entertainment and amusements, retail, toiletries and cosmetics, travel and hotels and resorts, and business services.

Throughout the world kinds of advertisers and even specific names are remarkably constant. Eighty-seven of America's largest 100 advertisers are multinationals. The main advertisers in Australia include Unilever and Philip Morris; in Brazil, British-American Tobacco and Ford; in France, IBM and Renault; in Japan, Toyota and Matsushita; in Germany, Volkswagen, Procter and Gamble, and Henkel; in the United Kingdom, Procter and Gamble, Mars, and Kellogg.

It is not necessary to be very cynical to conclude after a look through the names of major advertisers and products that the less obvious the need for any item the greater **its** dependence on advertising. Traditionally, the big advertisers are the producers of what are known as FMCGs—Fast Moving Consumer Goods—in other words smallish items that frequently have to be rebought such as cigarettes, candy, potato chips, and soap powder.

The world's largest advertiser remains a traditional FMCG company, Procter and Gamble. The scale of its advertising, and **its** consequent impact throughout the world, is truly awesome. It markets eighty-three brand-name items in thirty-eight product categories in the United States and 140 foreign countries. Among **them** are Camay, Ivory and Zest soaps, Pampers diapers, Head and Shoulders shampoo, Crest toothpaste, Vicks cold remedies, and Vidal Sassoon products. By the beginning of the eighties, Procter and Gamble was already buying anything from 18,000 to 20,000 thirty-second commercial spots on American TV alone. But Procter and Gamble's influence does not stop there. The wrapping around its messages is as important as the messages themselves, and the company also produces 1,000 daytime hours of its own TV each year plus miniseries such as *The Holocaust* and *Marco Polo* that have filled screens throughout the world. P&G's involvement with program content is far from new. The company invented the soap opera as a vehicle for its commercials and virtually built daytime radio for the networks.

Ever-increasing internationalism is one of the dominant features of the advertising world. It is possible to step off an airplane in any nation of the world and see the **effect.** Pick up a paper in Turkey, say, and odds are that there will be an ad for Marlboro or Lowenbrau; switch on the TV and the commercial may feature Mercedes or Mitsubishi. If products can be internationalized, there are economies of scale (including ones to be made in advertising). A drinks advertiser ran through products that were now "international": jeans, T-shirts, sports shoes, soft drinks, power tools, credit cards, fast food . . . He suggested to me that we note down as many individual brands as came to mind in five minutes. The list was formidable . . . You could walk into any town certainly anywhere in Europe and find that **such words** were part of the everyday currency and their advertising part of the routine advertising.

Task 1

Put these ideas in the order [1–4] that they appear in the text.

[ ] The more widely a product is advertised, the better value for money it becomes for the company.
[ ] World advertising is dominated by a relatively small number of large companies.
[ ] TV and radio programs are sometimes produced only to capture an audience for advertisements.
[ ] If a product is truly necessary, heavy advertising is not.

Task 2

Which of these are the main points of the text [M] and which are supplementary points [S]?

[ ] Fast Moving Consumer Goods and vehicles are the most heavily advertised products.
[ ] The worldwide advertising industry is controlled by a few giant multinationals whose influence is vast.
[ ] The same products are being advertised in more and more countries, which allows companies to make economies of scale.
[ ] The largest companies not only dominate advertising but also are beginning to control program content.

Task 3

What do these words, printed in **bold** in the text, refer to?

its (para. 3)
its (para. 4)
them (para. 4)
effect (para. 5)
such words (para. 5)

Adapted from Eric Clark, *The Want Makers* (Harmondsworth: Penguin Books, 1990), 29–33, 42.

Task 4

Look at the following words from the text and decide which is the correct definition in that context.

breakdown (para. 1): **1**. failure of a system, plan, or discussion; **2**. a description of something in terms of its separate parts; **3**. sudden failure of a machine

remedies (para. 1): **1**. ways of curing pains; **2**. ways of correcting things that are wrong

wrapping (para. 4): **1**. decorative material used to present something attractively; **2**. a piece of material used to cover and protect something

vehicle (para. 4): **1**. a machine that carries people or things from place to place; **2**. something that you use in order to achieve a particular purpose

odds (para. 5): **1**. difference; **2**. small articles of little value; **3**. probability

currency (para. 5): **1**. symbols that are in common use in a country; **2**. the system of money that is used in a country

Task 5

Paragraph 5 talks about the internationalization of products and advertising. In what ways do we as consumers benefit from this? In what ways do we lose out? List your ideas in the following chart.

Benefits	Losses

The Hidden Persuaders

Prereading

Look at the two advertisements. What is each one advertising? In each case what makes the advertisement effective?

To their last investment manager they were Findlay, Mr S. and Mrs C. 63201.
To us they're Simon, Caroline and Jamie... and on holiday till Thursday week.
As the Findlays have found, there's a lot more to personal service than simply being on a first name basis with our clients.
We've made it our business to get to know their lifestyle and their goals and the fact that, for the foreseeable future, they'll be investing in school fees rather than offshore funds.
Because only by knowing their aims can we meet their expectations.
So, while we're immensely proud of the way our market expertise has consistently provided exemplary financial performance, we're prouder still of how our personal service is helping the Findlays achieve their aspirations.
For further information contact Mark Smith on 071-956 6600.
KLEINWORT BENSON
PRIVATE BANK
To meet your needs better we get to know you better
Kleinwort Benson Private Bank is a Division of Kleinwort Benson Investment Management Limited, member of the Stock Exchange and IMRO. Marketing Group Associate – Kleinwort Benson Unit Trusts Limited. The characters in this advertisement are purely fictional.

Take a break from the shopping. Have a cappuccino.

Treat yourself. Try a white chocolate Cappuccino,
or a Rum Truffle, or any other of the chocolates from our celebrated Continental Selection.
You don't have to buy a whole box at Thorntons. But you might want to.

Thorntons

Chocolate Heaven Since 1911

Reading

Look at task 1 below and then read through the text quickly, without using a dictionary. Advertising often appeals to us at subconscious levels, targeting our self-esteem, our ambitions, our dreams, and our secret desires. It also plays on our fears and secret anxieties, as Vance Packard illustrates in the following text.

(Opening paragraph missing—see task 1)

The smoking of cigarettes for many people had become deeply enmeshed in such guilt feelings, which had been generated in part presumably because the habit had been sternly repressed in childhood and partly from the genuine suspicion that cigarettes were coffin nails.

The investigators found many reasons why people continue to smoke despite their guilt feelings: they smoke to relieve tension, to express sociability, as a reward for effort, as an aid in anticipating stress, and as proof of conformity. Perhaps the major discovery, however, was that Americans smoke to prove they are people of virile maturity and potency. This is a psychological satisfaction sufficient to overcome health fears and withstand moral censure. As a result, cigarette advertising began to reflect these discoveries: many ads were showing people smoking under pressure or as a reward for tough jobs done, and the characters in many of the ads exuded virile maturity.

Meanwhile the producers of sugar-tooth items were confronting a public suffering from massive guilt feelings of another sort. Americans were starting to shun anything conspicuously sweet and sugary, suffering both persistent guilt feelings about indulging themselves and unease over the widely publicized dangers of overweight and tooth decay. The candymakers, losing customers in a "sticky market," sought advice from a motivational analyst. He mapped for them a strategy for getting us back to candy-munching on a mass basis. The real deep-down problem they had to cope with, he advised, was this guilt feeling about self-indulgence. One of the tactics he urged was to emphasize bite-size pieces within the present large-size candy packages. That would appeal to us as self-indulgence in moderation and give us the excuse we need to buy a bar of candy—"After all, I don't need to eat all of it, just a bite, then put the rest away."

One candymaking firm came up with another strategy: reward yourself. The theory behind this was that children get rewards of candy for being "a good little boy or girl." Thus at an early age candy becomes etched in young minds as a reward symbol. Armed with this insight, the candymaker began drumming out this message, "To make that tough job easier—you deserve M&M candy." According to the company, sales doubled in test areas.

Wine producers faced another sort of mass uneasiness when people were confronted with the product. The great number of wine types, the emphasis on good and bad years and the correct glass for each type added up to a situation that made prospective customers fearful and unhappy about buying a bottle of wine. A psychologist who looked into the problem for the wine merchants advised them to stop the esoteric nonsense and hammer across to the public that any wine is good no matter how you serve it; and that is essentially what they began doing, with considerable success.

Our relationship with banks is another area where we have a large variety of fears: fear of being rejected for a loan, fear of the banker finding out how untidy the family financial affairs really are, or fear of disapproval. Researchers concluded that people subconsciously see their bank as a kind of parent, capable of scolding or withholding approval and constantly scrutinizing. With that in mind, an ad was designed showing a man standing at the door saying, "How I hated to open that door!" and then relating his story of the warm welcome he got. The banks' big handicap was their stern image of unemotional morality, which made us feel like unreliable adolescents.

As Ernest Dichter, a famous motivation analyst, said, "One of the main jobs of the advertiser in this conflict between pleasure and guilt is not so much to sell the product as to give moral permission to have fun without guilt."

Task 1

Choose the best opening paragraph for the text from these three.

a. Advertising agencies have spent millions of dollars funding research into motivational studies. From this research they have discovered that one of the main reasons people continue to buy cigarettes, candy, wine, and other products and services is because they suffer from guilt and anxiety.

b. Tobacco smoking, candy, wine, and banks are the four main areas where advertisers have successfully used our feelings of guilt and fear to persuade us to buy their goods and services. The techniques used vary little from product to product.

c. In learning to sell to our subconscious, advertising agencies also began to explore our miseries and self-doubts. They concluded that the sale of billions of dollars' worth of products hinged on successfully manipulating or coping with guilt feelings, fears, anxieties, hostilities, loneliness, and inner tensions.

Adapted from Vance Packard, *The Hidden Persuaders* (Harmondsworth: Penguin Books, 1957, 1981), 54–65.

Task 2

Write questions for these answers. Refer back to paragraphs 2 and 3 of the text to help you.

because they had been told it was bad when they were young
by showing virile men smoking
people who are under stress and tension
they didn't mention it's bad for your health

Task 3

Complete this chart with information about people's fears and the advertising techniques that exploit them.

	Fears	Advertising Techniques
candy		
wine		
banks		

Task 4

Scan the text and make two lists, one of words connected with psychology and one of words connected with warfare.

Psychology	Warfare
subconscious	targeting

Task 5

a. This text was first written in 1957. Which points do you think are still true today and which do you think have changed?

____

____

____

____

b. Look again at the advertising techniques mentioned in the text. Do you think any of them are deceitful? Which (if any)?

____

____

____

____

Fluency Activities

Matching

Look at the advertisements below. Each relies on one of the following four human feelings in order to sell the product advertised. Match the feelings to the ads.

status
nostalgia
guilt
physical attraction

KEEP THE HOMEFIRE BURNING
Capture the mood · Create the glow · Re-kindle your yesterdays · With the fuel of today
With clean smokeless HOMEFIRE · For maximum heat · And minimum waste
For longer burning · On cold winter nights · Brings people together · Drives the cold away
Homefire
Look out for the gold and black bags at petrol stations, garden centres and corner shops. Or order HOMEFIRE direct from your Coal Merchant.
Homefire – all our yesterdays from today's fuel

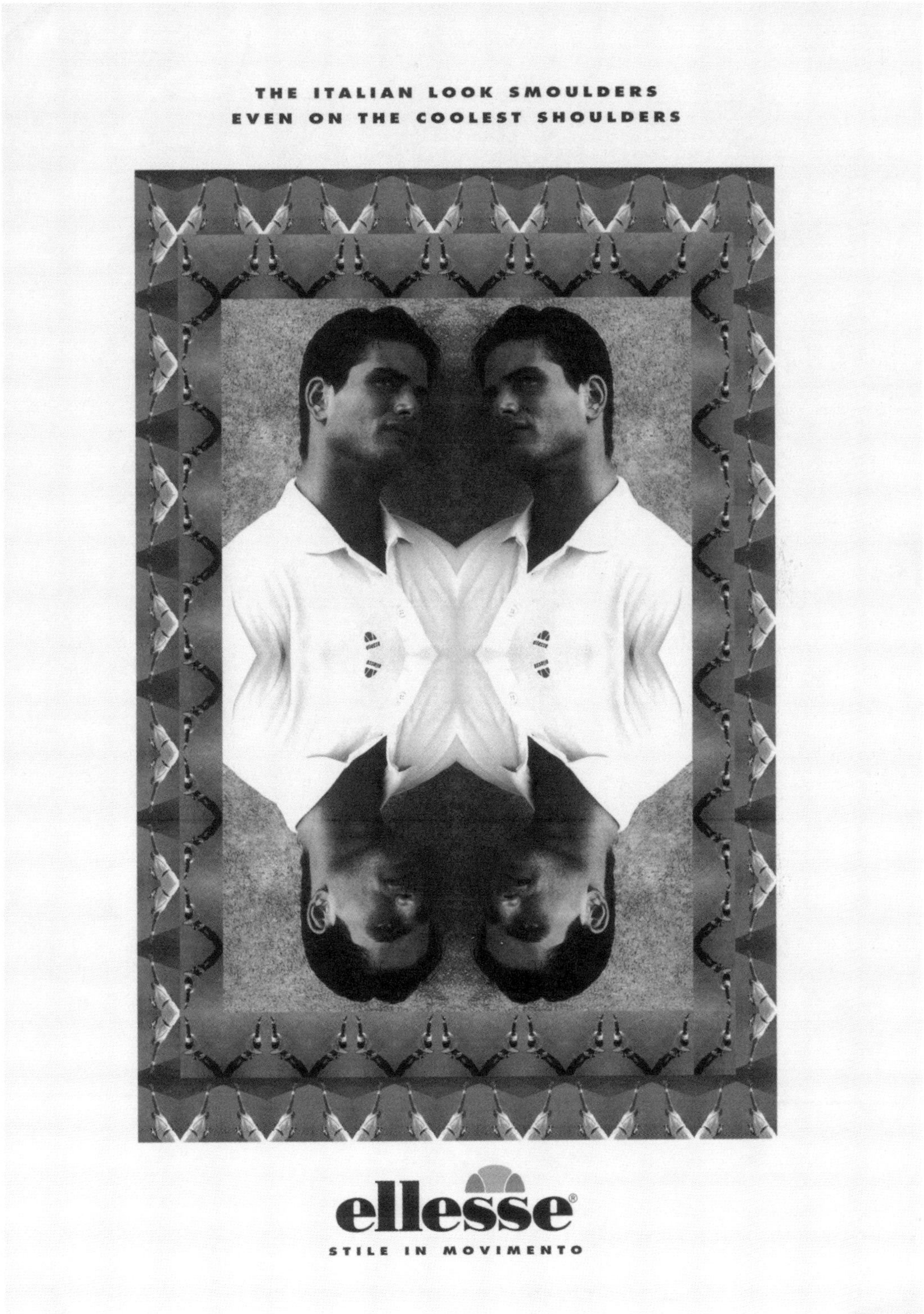
THE ITALIAN LOOK SMOULDERS
EVEN ON THE COOLEST SHOULDERS
ellesse®
STILE IN MOVIMENTO

For a so-called small car, the new 5-door Corsa CDX delivers some big surprises. Like over 2½ inches more rear legroom and almost 1½ inches more rear headroom than its biggest selling competitor.

Along with a boot of class-leading capaciousness. (More than big enough to house the latest creations from Milan's finest fashion designers.)

Not that the CDX isn't already loaded with luxury items.

Electric front windows and mirrors, a tilt/slide sunroof, power steering, full-size driver and passenger airbags, 6 speaker radio/CD player and an

CAR SHOWN IS THE CORSA CDX 1.4i 16v 5 DOOR HATCH AT £11,970. PRICE CORRECT AT TIME OF GOING TO PRESS AND INCLUDES VAUXHALL'S RECOMMENDED ON-THE-ROAD PACKAGE £450 AND

'Engine Deadlock' immobiliser are all already on board.

ABS braking, a 4-speed automatic gearbox and sumptuous leather trim are extra cost options which can be added at the drop of a hat. Whilst under its pretty bonnet lies a potent 90HP 1.4i 16v ECOTEC engine.

And the price tag for such a desirable, well-designed little number? £11,970 on the road. So why not contact your local Vauxhall dealer or telephone 0800 444 200 and try one for size?

THE CORSA CDX FROM VAUXHALL

12 MONTHS ROAD FUND LICENCE £135. OPTIONAL LEATHER TRIM AVAILABLE FROM JUNE PRODUCTION. A RADIO/CASSETTE PLAYER IS OPTIONAL AT NO EXTRA COST TO REPLACE RADIO/CD PLAYER.

Language Analysis 1

Look at the word "pure" in this ad. What does it mean in the sentence: "Colour was never so pure"?

Sensiq is a new range of cosmetics specially formulated to be gentle on your skin.

Our philosophy is 'just say no.'

No to lanolin. No to fragrance. No to testing on animals.

Nothing but pure colour.

New Fine Lining Eye Pen £3.99. Duo Shadow Silk £2.49.

You'll find them at selected Boots stores and other leading chemists. For your nearest stockist call 0800 289 796.

Which words work in the same way in these ads?

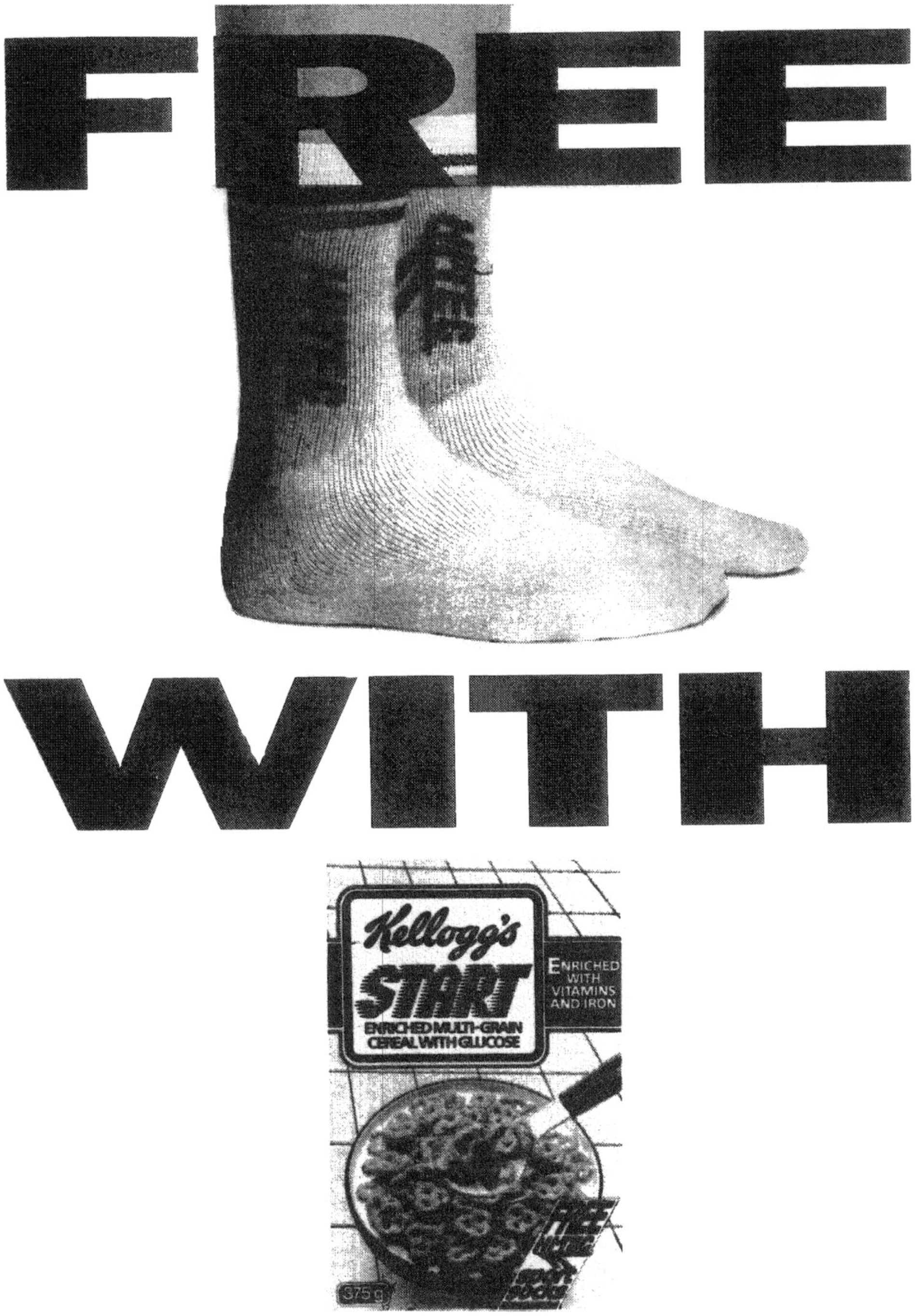

Whatever your sport, you'll enjoy wearing these great socks from Hi-Tec and they are Absolutely free (just contribute 20p towards postage). Available in 2 sizes.

Simply cut out this token and collect 3 more from special packs of Kellogg's Start. See back of pack for details.

Presenting
NATURAL instincts
Inspired by Nature ... Naturally
Introducing Natural Instincts, the first haircolour with a unique blend of Aloe Vera, Jojoba, Ginseng and plant derived conditioners in a Botanicolor complex that is actually good for your hair.
Natural Instincts will enhance and enliven the colour nature gave you adding complementary colour tones to bring out the full beauty of your hair.
The fresh, floral fragrance is gentle to your senses. While the conditioning formula is so gentle to your hair, it's left better conditioned than before you coloured it. In just 10 minutes!
New Natural Instincts from Clairol
CLAIROL
NATURAL instincts
Conditioning Colourant with Natural Ingredients
Contains Aloe, Jojoba and Ginseng
12 Toasted Almond - Light Golden Brown
ENHANCES NATURAL COLOUR, ADDS SHINE
NO AMMONIA, LOW PEROXIDE
GENTLE ACTION, LASTING RESULTS
BLENDS AWAY GREY
CLAIROL

Does the next ad say that smoking marijuana *will* damage your lungs, impair brain functions . . . ?

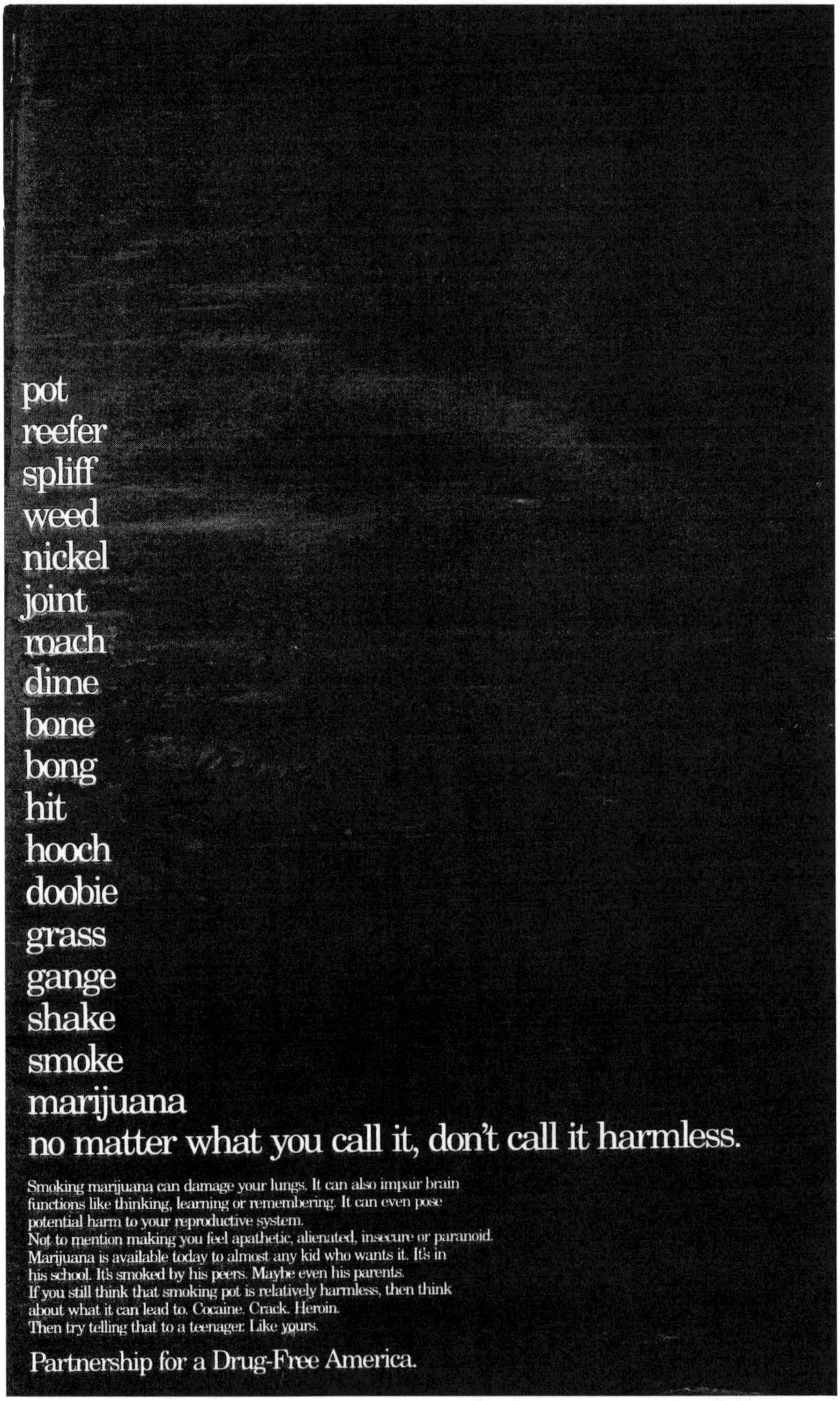

Which word in the ad below has a similar effect?

The next ad mentions a test. Who organized the test? On how many people? Where? Do you think this test was conducted scientifically?

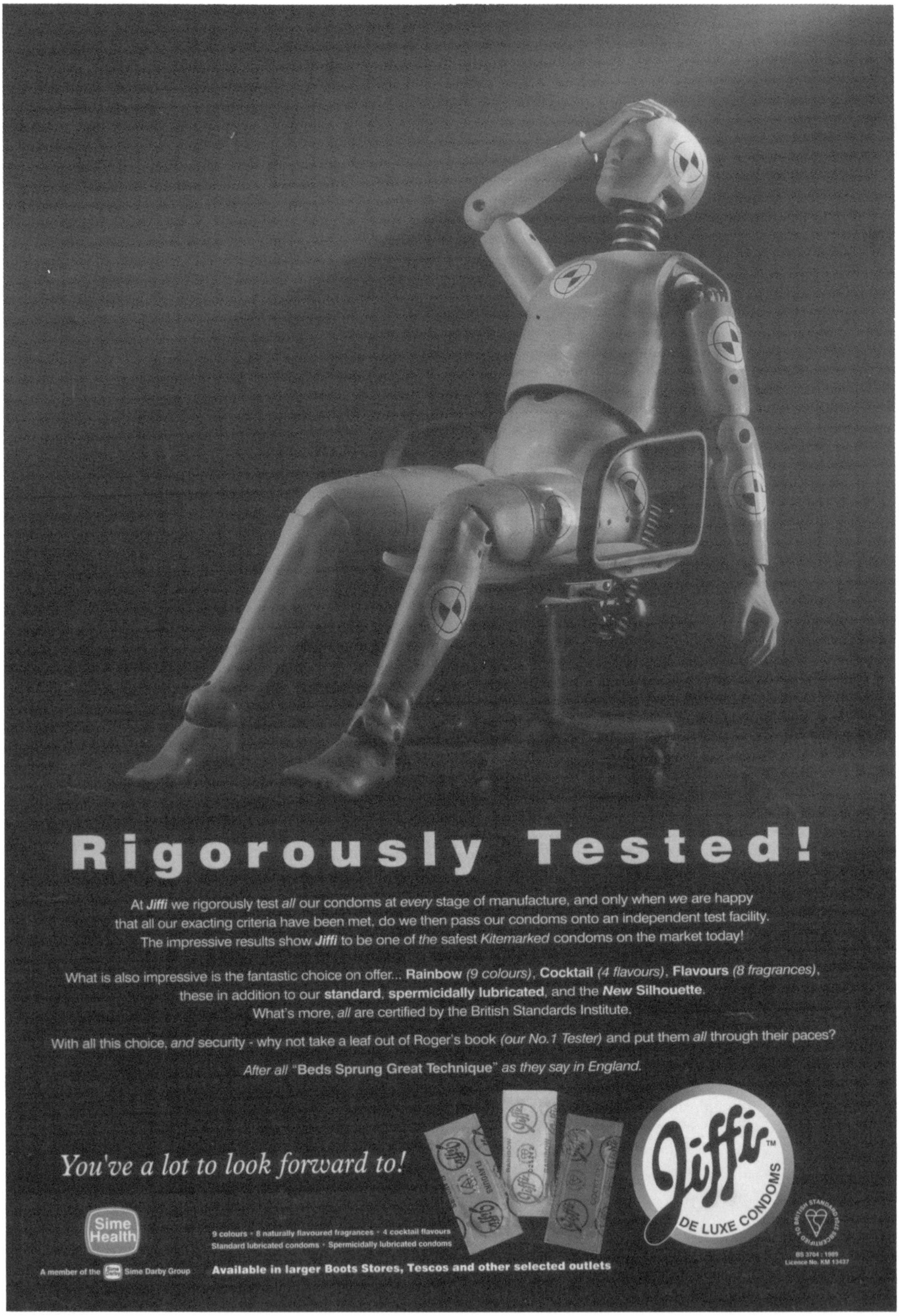
Rigorously Tested!
At Jiffi we rigorously test all our condoms at every stage of manufacture, and only when we are happy that all our exacting criteria have been met, do we then pass our condoms onto an independent test facility. The impressive results show Jiffi to be one of the safest Kitemarked condoms on the market today!
What is also impressive is the fantastic choice on offer... Rainbow (9 colours), Cocktail (4 flavours), Flavours (8 fragrances), these in addition to our standard, spermicidally lubricated, and the New Silhouette. What's more, all are certified by the British Standards Institute.
With all this choice, and security - why not take a leaf out of Roger's book (our No.1 Tester) and put them all through their paces?
After all "Beds Sprung Great Technique" as they say in England.
You've a lot to look forward to!
Jiffi™ DE LUXE CONDOMS
Sime Health
A member of the Sime Darby Group
9 colours · 8 naturally flavoured fragrances · 4 cocktail flavours
Standard lubricated condoms · Spermicidally lubricated condoms
Available in larger Boots Stores, Tescos and other selected outlets
BS 3704 : 1989
Licence No. KM 13437

How is the following ad similar? (Look at the part beginning "Premium posturepedic.")

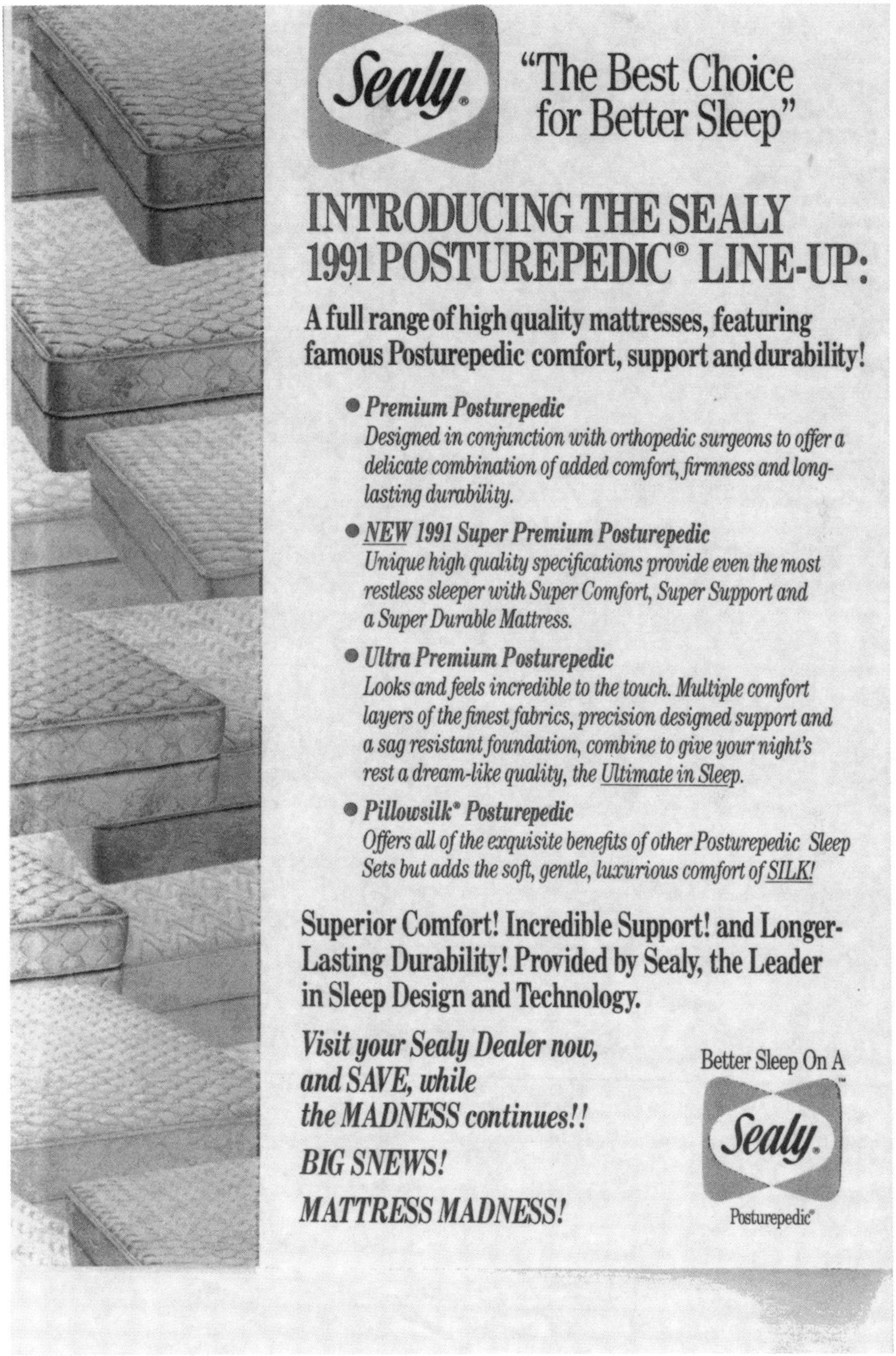

Language Analysis 2

Clever wordplay is a technique that helps fix a product in the reader's mind. Pick out and explain the word plays in these ads.

Photos by Peter Rauter

HITACHI
DEAF LEOPARD
HITACHI 4-band stereo receiver, with 32-track programmable CD, twin cassettes (one with auto reverse), 3-band graphic equalizer, 80 watts PMP output, and a deafeningly loud acoustic SuperWoofer system. THE HITACHI SUPERWOOFER.
YOU'LL · NEVER · REGRET · BUYING · HITACHI

The lighter cider life.
Frés
CIDRE BLOND
THE NEW CIDER SPRITZER

Read your lips.
One sip will
tell it all.
And that's a
promise
not subject
to change.
SMIRNOFF
PIERRE SMIRNOFF
SMIRNOFF® VODKA 40 & 50% Alc. by Vol., distilled from premium grain. © 1990 Ste. Pierre Smirnoff FLS (Division of Heublein, Inc.) Hartford, CT · Made in U.S.A.

Use Your Own Judgment

Now look back at all the advertisements in this unit. Can you spot any other techniques that help sell the products?
Are similar techniques to the ones presented in these activities used in ads in your first language?

Creativity

Imagine you are creating a magazine advertisement for a new product. Decide the following.

what kind of product (give it a name!)
the people you will target

Now design an effective advertisement and show it to the class.

Project

Find examples of effective advertisements in magazines and newspapers; bring them to the next class and explain the techniques used.

Debate

Divide yourselves into two teams (For and Against) and brainstorm as many arguments as you can. Then either split up your arguments among the team and each side take turns presenting and defending your case, or pair off with a member of the opposing team and argue it out face to face. Argue either for or against the following statement.

The influence of advertising has become so harmful that it should be banned.

Teacher's Notes and Answer Key

The Want Makers

Prereading. Colgate = toothpaste, United States; *American Express* = credit cards, United States; *Chivas Regal* = Scotch whisky, United States/United Kingdom; *Canon* = cameras, Japan; *Pepsi* = soft drinks, United States; *Heineken* = beer, Holland; *Kodak* = film, United States; *Marlboro* = cigarettes, United States; *Nescafe* = coffee, Switzerland; *Mercedes* = cars, Germany; *Lego* = toys, Denmark; *McDonald's* = hamburger shops, United States; *Levis* = jeans, United States; *KitKat* = candy, United Kingdom/ Switzerland; *Sony Walkman* = personal cassette player, Japan; *Kellogg's* = breakfast cereal, United States; *Lux* = soap, United States; *Reebok* = sports shoes, United States; *Contac* = cold remedy, United States.

Task 1. 4, 1, 3, 2

Task 2. S, M, S, S

Task 3. its = the item; *its* = Procter and Gamble/P&G's advertising; *them* = brand-name items; *the effect* = of internationalism in advertising; *such words* = the brand names in his list

Task 4. breakdown = 2; *remedies* = 1; *wrapping* = 1; *vehicle* = 2; *odds* = 3; *currency* = 1

The Hidden Persuaders

Prereading. One advertises banking, the other chocolates. Their effectiveness depends on many things but most obviously an appeal to the personal (caring for you) for the bank ad and the visual-verbal confusion over the word *cappuccino* for the chocolate ad. Readers expect it to mean coffee break, but the picture says chocolate.

Task 1. The original text used c.

Task 2. Suitable questions are:

Why do many people feel guilty about smoking?
How do cigarette advertisers overcome our health fears?
What kind of people are tempted to smoke?
What did cigarette advertisers fail to mention?

Task 3. Candy: overindulgence, overweight, tooth decay—bite-size pieces, reward yourself; *wine:* esoteric nonsense of wine types, years, and glasses—any wine, served any way, is good; *banks:* being rejected for a loan, untidy family finances, disapproval—banks are like parents, so make them kind and welcoming

Task 4. Psychology: subconscious, self-doubts, manipulating, guilt, anxieties, inner tensions, repressed, sociability, conformity, motivational analyst, reward symbol, psychologist; *Warfare:* strategy, tactics, armed, drumming out, confronted, hammer across, conflict.

Fluency Activities

Matching. physical attraction—Ellesse; status—Vauxhall; nostalgia—Homefire; guilt—ACTIONAID.

Language Analysis 1. There is of course no such thing as "pure color"—pure is used as a buzzword, having no denominational meaning but having a high connotational value. "Natural" in the Clairol ad (also can something natural really be "new"?), and "Free" in the Kellogg's ad are similar—manufactured hair colorants are not natural, and nothing produced by a commercial company is really free.

The marijuana ad only says smoking "can" damage your lungs, etc., not that it necessarily will. Blisteze "fights" infection (not the same as overcoming it) and "helps" your lips to heal (not quite the same as "heals your lips").

The Jiffi condoms bear the Kitemark, which guarantees a certain standard of manufacture (British Standard 3704), but there is no evidence in the ad that Jiffi's own testing procedure is to more rigorous standards, though this may be the impression that readers get.

The Sealy mattress ad uses the phrase "designed in conjunction with orthopedic surgeons" in a similar way. Does this make their beds somehow better than those designed by a "good bed designer"?

Language Analysis 2. Hitachi: The musical group Def Leppard was well known in the late 1980s for playing heavy metal music so loudly that it could deafen listeners; *Comfort:* this is a fabric conditioner that can obviously even soften a hedgehog's spines; "rough" meaning not soft and "rough it" meaning live under primitive conditions; *Frés:* this ad uses a verbal pun, "the lighter side of life," meaning comedy and laughter illustrated by a visual pun—a boxer wearing glove puppets on his hands; *Smirnoff:* a pun on President Reagan's famous promise, "Read my lips," plus "one sip will tell it all," which is juxtaposing "read" and "tell" and "lips" and "sip."

Use Your Own Judgment. This is an open-ended activity. See what learners come up with. There is a lot of wordplay in the ads, but many of the instances require a deep cultural knowledge to be understandable. For instance, "Keep the homefires burning" was a British propaganda phrase in World War I, and the Jiffi advertisement is actually a spoof on an earlier advertisement for BMW cars!

Unit 6
Biosphere Blues

Murder in the Rain Forest

Prereading

You are going to read a text about the destruction of tropical forests. Make a list of ten to fifteen words that you think might appear in the text.

____

____

____

____

Reading

Look at task 1 below and then read through the text quickly, without using a dictionary.

Rain forests and rain go together. If the forest goes, then so does the rain. That is why the destruction of the Amazon jungle and the murder of Francisco Mendes are bad news for the whole world.

The climatic argument is simple. Dark colors absorb sunlight. Therefore the air over a rain forest is cooler than the air over a desert. In cooler air, water vapor is more likely to fall as rain. Over a light, sandy, reflecting desert it is less likely to fall. This is called the albedo effect. This means the rich habitats get richer, and the poor get poorer. The desert is the final poverty trap.

The tropical forests are the richest habitats in creation; most of the world's 30 million forms of life live in the forests of the Amazon. But the richness is, like most wealth, precarious. The soil below the forest is surprisingly poor. When the tropical forests are burned and cleared for cattle ranching—to keep the hamburger industry producing the quarter-pounders at low prices—the next season's rain starts washing away the nutrients from the soil. Within a few years the basic soil bakes into a bricklike, water resistant skin.

Water runs off this skin; rain forests are great sponges, absorbing the season's rains and letting go of the water gradually through the dry seasons. Once the forests are gone, the rainwater runs instantly into the rivers, taking the topsoil with it and bringing destructive floods to the rich farmland downstream. After a while, according to the albedo effect, the rains should start to fail: a desert is born.

This creates another problem. The great deserts and the polar ice sheets and the oceans are all parts of the world's weather machine. So are the rain forests. Nobody knows what would happen to the world's climate patterns if something as big as the Amazon basin turned from rain forest into desert.

Then there is the greenhouse effect: the warming of the world as the quantity of carbon dioxide (CO_2) in the atmosphere increases, thus trapping the sun's heat. The carbon dioxide comes from the burning of coal and oil by the industrial world and also, ironically, from the burning of the forests themselves—the very forests that should be absorbing the CO_2 (plants use carbon dioxide to grow and give it off as they die or burn). As the world warms up, the oceans will expand and the ice caps will melt and the seas will rise.

Francisco Mendes, a Brazilian rubber tapper, organized rural people, rubber tappers and forest Indians, to protect the rain forest against the people who were burning it away to make cattle ranches. In 1988, Mendes spoke out against several big international companies that were profiting from this clearing of the jungles. In the week before Christmas, Mendes was shot in the chest and killed at his own home in the town of Xapuri. Police failed to capture the two men seen running away. His death should be a warning to us all.

Task 1

Decide whether these statements are true [T] or false [F].

[ ] The albedo effect explains why the rain forests are being cleared.
[ ] The trees protect the soil of the jungle and prevent the destruction of farmland beyond it.
[ ] Because the world is warming up, the amount of CO_2 in the atmosphere is increasing.
[ ] Cattle ranches can only survive for a few years on deforested land.
[ ] Francisco Mendes was killed because he was a threat to somebody's quick commercial profits.

Adapted from Tim Radford, "Murder in the Rainforests," *Guardian*, 5 January 1989.

Task 2

What happens after a rain forest is cleared by burning? Look at paragraphs 3 and 4 and complete the following sentences to explain the process.

The rain forests are cleared by burning.

Over the next few rainy seasons ______________________________

Over the next few dry seasons ______________________________

Each year, the air becomes hotter and drier.

Each year, the rains ______________________________

Eventually______________________________

Task 3

Find words in the text that mean the following.

natural homes of plants and animals (para. 2)
not stable, insecure (para. 3)
natural chemicals that feed plants and help them to grow (para. 3)
Arctic and Antarctic (para. 5)
someone who collects the juice from rubber trees (para. 7)

Task 4

Using the statements below, complete the flowchart to explain the greenhouse effect (para. 6).

The seas rise.
Too much CO_2 collects in the atmosphere.
Factories, etc., produce CO_2.
Oceans expand.
The sun's heat is trapped instead of going into space.
The ice caps melt.
The burning of forests produces CO_2.

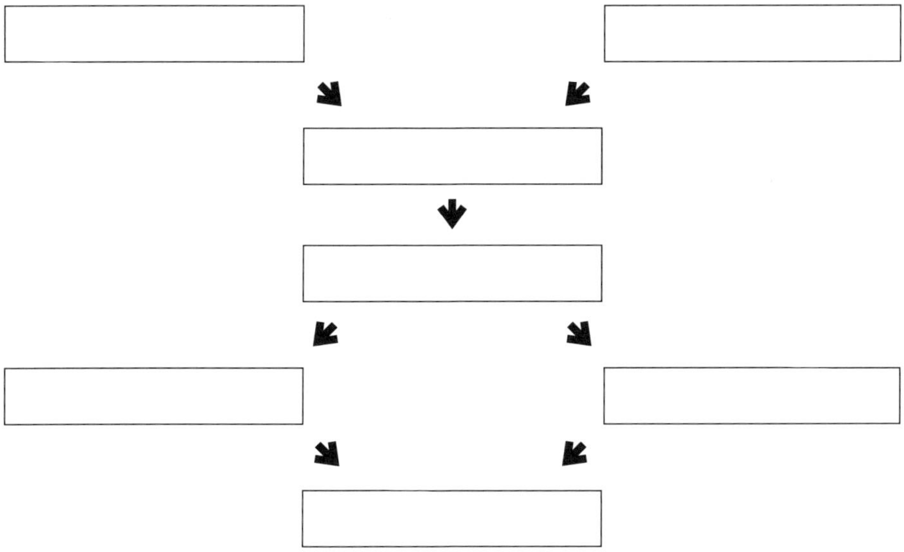

Task 5

What will be the consequences of the warming world and the rising seas?
Write down as many ideas as you can.

Task 6

Who was responsible for Francisco Mendes's death?
Why should his death be "a warning to us all"?

Cleaner Cars for California

Prereading

Answer the following questions in pairs.

Do you or your family have a car?	☐ Yes ☐ No
If Yes: Does it run on . . . ☐ diesel? ☐ leaded gas? ☐ unleaded gas? Does it have a catalytic converter? ☐ Yes ☐ No ☐ Not known How many people are in the care most times it is used? ☐ 1 ☐ 2 ☐ 3 ☐ 4 ☐ 5 or more	If No: How do you get around? ☐ bus ☐ shuttle bus ☐ taxi ☐ subway ☐ bicycle ☐ on foot ☐ motorcycle What could be done to improve the area's transport system? ____________________ ____________________

Reading

Look at task 1 below and then read through the text quickly, without using a dictionary.

California has a problem. Each day, its vehicles consume 25 million gallons of gasoline and contribute to one of the world's worst cases of air pollution. Carbon monoxide, nitrogen oxides, and unburned hydrocarbons are among the poisons produced in a car engine, and in sunny weather the last two combine to produce ozone, a gas that interferes with the respiratory system.

Until the 1970s, the American car manufacturers had maintained that nothing could be done about these emissions. Meanwhile large cities in the United States were choking under thick brown smogs that hospitalized thousands. But then Richard "Catalyst" Klimisch discovered a way of chemically transforming most of these harmful emissions into more benign gases—and the rest is history. Since 1975, all new cars have been sold with catalytic converters built into their exhaust systems, and the improvement in the quality of the air has been appreciated by everybody who breathes it.

A happy ending? Not quite. There are still some pre-1975 automobiles in operation on California's highways—but more significant is the relentless growth in the car population. There are now eight million cars in Greater Los Angeles, and, in Orange County, 38 per cent of adults own three or more vehicles. Catalysts still allow some pollution to escape into the air, so the sheer number of cars in Los Angeles means that pollution levels are once again up to dangerously high levels. Smog has returned, and air pollution levels in the city regularly exceed the legal maximum. So Californians are looking beyond petroleum to alternative fuels in their crusade against smog. Cars can now be made to run on ethanol and methanol, and then there are electric cars—or even hydrogen-powered cars. All of these clean-running technologies have great potential for cutting pollution without infringing upon personal mobility.

There is a striking contrast between the American and European approaches to solving the problems of transport versus the environment. Whereas in Europe one tends to look beyond cars to areas such as the promotion of public transport or more efficient land-use planning, in the United States most proposals are related to improving the environmental friendliness of the automobile. Why? Because this is car culture, where everything is Drive-Thru: cinemas, banks, restaurants—Los Angeles even has a drive-thru church. For this reason, alternative fuels are seen as the solution to the air quality crisis in California. Citizens will be able to continue living in their cars with little or no disruption to their present lifestyle. The "LA Plan," a radical set of antipollution measures, proposes to phase out altogether gas-driven cars in Los Angeles by 2008.

But there are growing concerns that such a scheme would simply move the pollution into someone else's backyard. The giant methanol refineries that would be required produce large volumes of airborne toxins and from a greenhouse perspective could create more carbon dioxide than the present generation of autos in Los Angeles. The same applies to electric vehicles: policymakers talk glibly about "zero-emission" cars, but "zero-emissions" is hardly an apt description for the coal-burning power stations needed to provide the sparks. Renewable auto fuels are a different matter. Electricity produced from hydroelectric, solar, or wind power could run cleaner cars; likewise ethanol or methanol produced from vegetation that is replanted afterward.

The Californians have opted for a giant "technical fix" to ease their environmental problems. In terms of reducing their dependence on the automobile they have done nothing, and the long-term trends toward even greater mobility, urban sprawl, and energy profligacy are wholly unsustainable. Technical solutions can be very effective in the short term but do not address deeper maladies such as the Californians' addiction to the automobile, and there is a real danger that the rest of the world, lemminglike, will be led down this same road to catastrophe.

Adapted from an article by Peter Hughes in the *New Democrat International,* November/December 1990, 4–5.

Task 1

Which paragraph tells you about the following?

[ ] problems with alternative fuels
[ ] the invention of the catalytic converter
[ ] how "car culture" restricts strategies for fighting air pollution
[ ] the inadequacy of the Californian strategy
[ ] some effects of poisonous exhaust gases
[ ] the limits of catalysts and the interest in nonpolluting fuels

Task 2

Look at these four statements. In each case, all the answers are true, but which of the three choices gives the main point of the text?

1. The catalytic converter
   a. is now fitted into all new American cars
   b. was a major invention in the fight against pollution
   c. cannot be a long-term answer to the air pollution problem
2. Cars running on alternative fuels
   a. are much cleaner than gas-driven cars
   b. are not as clean as they first appear
   c. are strongly supported in the "LA Plan"
3. The Californians' dependence on cars
   a. could be a danger to the rest of the world
   b. is at the root of the Californian air pollution problem
   c. determines their lifestyle
4. In contrast to Californians, Europeans
   a. plan their land-use more efficiently
   b. are promoting the use of public transport
   c. realise that technical solutions alone are not enough

Task 3

Find these phrases in the text. Rewrite them using other words, so that their meaning is clear.

hospitalized thousands (para. 2)

the rest is history (para. 2)

____

____

environmental friendliness (para. 4)

____

____

living in their cars (para. 4)

____

____

into someone else's backyard (para. 5)

____

____

provide the sparks (para. 5)

____

____

Task 4

Complete this crossword puzzle by using words from the text.

Down

1. chemicals that poison people, animals, or plants (para. 5)
2. poisonous gases that build up over a city (para. 2)
3. unplanned and untidy city growth over a large area (two words—para. 6)
4. a long campaign in support of something you strongly believe in (para. 3)

Across

4. being unable to breathe properly (para. 2)
5. too damaging to continue for much longer (para. 6)
6. gradually withdraw something from use (two words—para. 4)

Task 5

These statements are inaccurate in some way. Explain what is wrong with them.

Catalytic converters make car exhaust gases safe.

Changing to electric cars would solve the smog problem.

The causes and solutions of the car emission problem are similar in California and in Europe.

38% of the adults in Orange County contribute more to its air pollution problem than the other 62%!

Task 6

Discuss the following questions with your partner, using your own knowledge and judgment to answer them.

a. In paragraph 3 the writer mentions hydrogen-powered cars. He does not mention them again in paragraph 5. Why not?
b. What is his preferred solution to the car emissions problem?
c. Does his dislike of the automobile seem unreasonable to you? Why (not)?

Fluency Activities

Sharing World Knowledge

Look at this map. Identify the environmental threats represented by the symbols and fill in the key below. The threats are: air pollution, ozone depletion, acid rain, desertification, deforestation, radiation, and toxic waste.

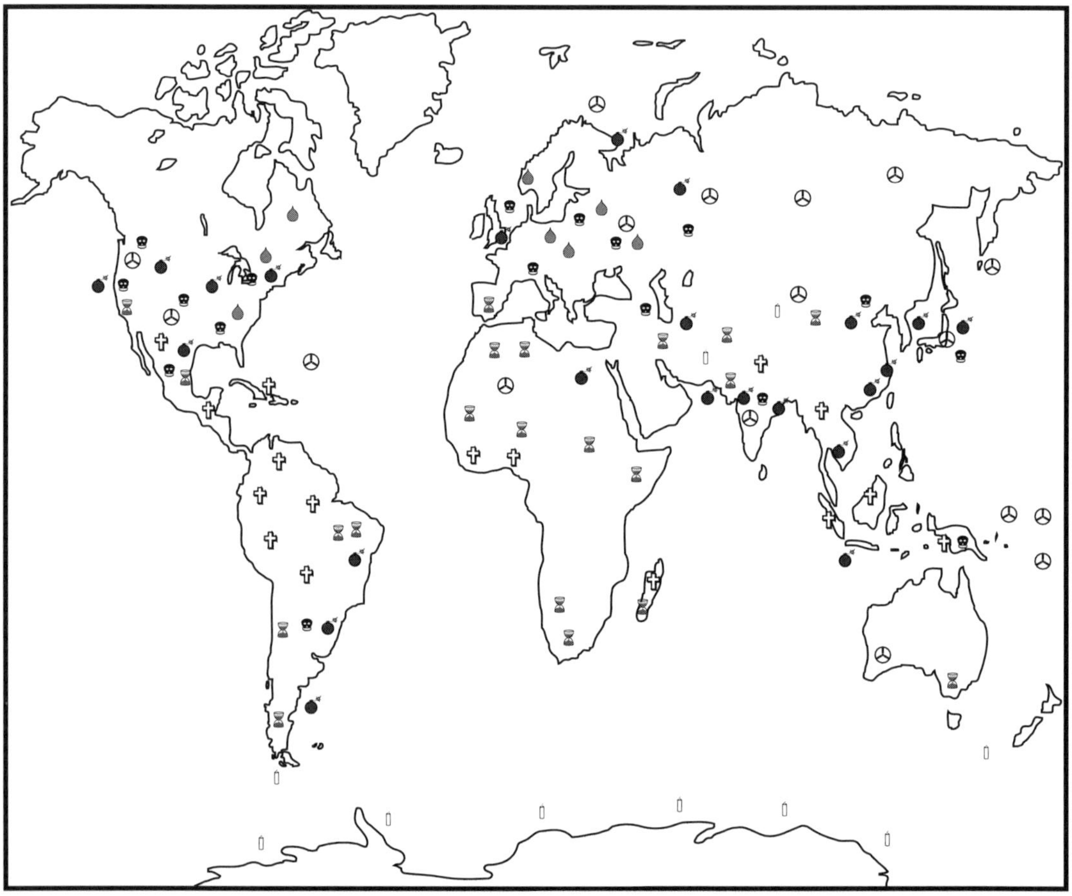

Key

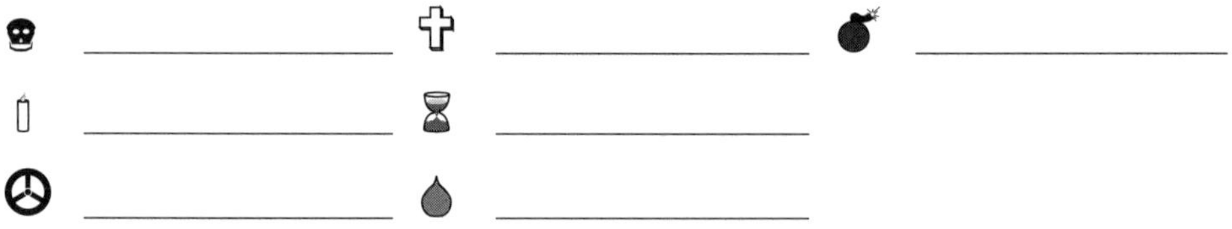

What other environmental threats do you know of?

Data derived from Judith Mackay, *The State of Health Atlas* (London: Simon & Schuster, 1993); and Joni Seager, *The State of the Earth* (London: Unwin and Hyman, 1990).

Matching

Match the activities listed below with the environmental problems that they help to cause, as in the example. The problems are as follows.

a. acid rain
b. ozone depletion
c. air pollution
d. water pollution
e. toxic waste
f. global warming
g. soil erosion
h. tropical deforestation
i. nonrenewable resource depletion

> EXAMPLE: You drive a car with unleaded gasoline.
> c, f, i, possibly a

1. Farmers use chemical fertilizers on their crops.
2. You throw away button batteries from your camera.
3. A power plant uses coal for making electricity.
4. A construction company uses plywood molding to build a concrete wall.
5. You buy foam-filled furniture for your home.
6. Peasants farm the same poor-quality land year after year.

Ranking

What can be done to stop the destruction of the environment? Rank the following suggestions from [1], the one you support most, to [6], the one you like least.

[ ] raise the gasoline tax so it doubles the price of gas
[ ] cancel debts of Third World countries if they take action to protect their rain forests and other resources
[ ] make companies pay for disposal of the packaging waste they create when they sell products like beer cans to consumers
[ ] set up a huge international tree-planting program
[ ] spend much more money on research into renewable energy sources such as wind and solar power
[ ] make recycling of paper, metal, glass and recyclable plastics compulsory, with fines for people who don't

Compare and explain your rankings.

Brainstorm

How do YOU in your daily life contribute to the destruction of the environment? Confess all!

____

____

____

____

____

____

____

____

Personal Survey

Ask your partner the following questions and check [√] her/his answers.

1. Do you collect any of the following for recycling?
   - ☐ newspapers ☺
   - ☐ metal cans ☺
   - ☐ glass bottles ☺
   - ☐ plastic bottles ☺ ☺
2. Do you use spray cans?
   - ☐ no, none ☺ ☺
   - ☐ only ozone-friendly cans ☺
   - ☐ yes ☹
3. Do you have any jewelry or ornaments containing
   - ☐ coral? ☹ ☹
   - ☐ ivory? ☹ ☹
   - ☐ diamonds? ☹
   - ☐ gold? ☹
   - ☐ pearls?
4. When you make a short journey, do you usually
   - ☐ walk or cycle? ☺ ☺
   - ☐ go by car? ☹
   - ☐ use public transport? ☺
5. Do you buy your eggs
   - ☐ loose? ☺
   - ☐ in clear plastic boxes? ☹
   - ☐ in polystyrene boxes? ☹
   - ☐ in cardboard boxes?
6. Do you buy your fruit or vegetables
   - ☐ loose? ☺
   - ☐ prepacked? ☹
7. What kind of shopping bag do you use?
   - ☐ a cloth bag or a basket ☺ ☺
   - ☐ a plastic bag that you reuse ☺
   - ☐ a new plastic bag ☹
   - ☐ a paper bag
8. How many electrical appliances do you have in your kitchen?
   - ☐ 10 or more ☹
   - ☐ 5–9
   - ☐ less than 5 ☺
9. Do you use disposable food utensils or containers
   - ☐ often? ☹ ☹
   - ☐ rarely?
   - ☐ never? ☺
10. Do you heat or cool your home
    - ☐ naturally ☺ ☺
    - ☐ by coal, oil, gas, or electricity ☹
    - ☐ by solar panels ☺ ☺

Add up the number of ☺ and ☹ your partner scored. Deduct ☹ from ☺ and check your rating below.

10 to 17: Your way of life does little harm to our planet. Well done!

1 to 9: You are harming the Earth to some extent. Try harder!

0 to –7: You need to become aware of the damage you are causing. Think about it!

–8 to –14: You are an unthinking consumer of the Earth's limited resources. Change your lifestyle now!

Stop and Think

How many people over the age of 40 knew about the following things when they were children?

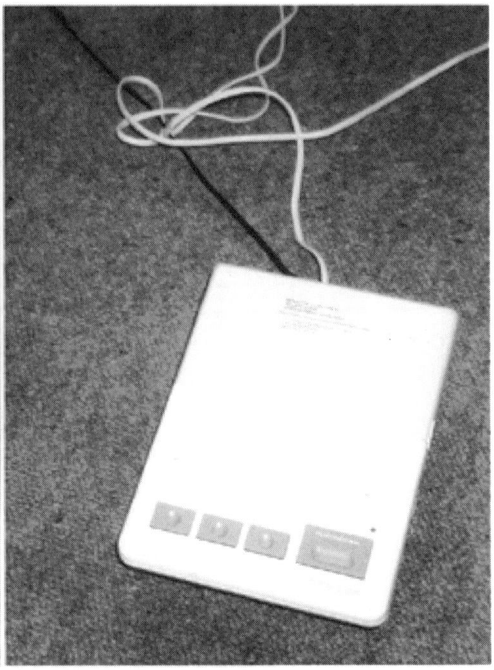

What does this tell you about the way we use the Earth's resources today?

Project

Look at the everyday products you use at home. Do the makers claim that they are "environmentally friendly"? Choose one or two products that you think are very environmentally friendly and one or two that you think are very bad for the environment. Bring them to your next class and be prepared to explain your choices.

Debate

Divide yourselves into two teams (For and Against) and brainstorm as many arguments as you can. Then either split up your arguments among the team and each side take turns presenting and defending your case, or pair off with a member of the opposing team and argue it out face to face. Argue either for or against the following statement.

The threat to the environment is the most important issue facing the world today.

Teacher's Notes and Answer Key

Murder in the Rain Forest

Task 1. F, T, F, T, T

Task 2. We think that the best answers are: *Over the next few rainy seasons* nutrients are washed from the soil. *Over the next few dry seasons* the soil bakes into a bricklike skin. *Each year the air becomes* hotter and drier. *Each year the rains become* rarer. *Eventually* a desert is born.

Task 3. habitats; precarious; nutrients; polar; rubber tapper

Task 4.

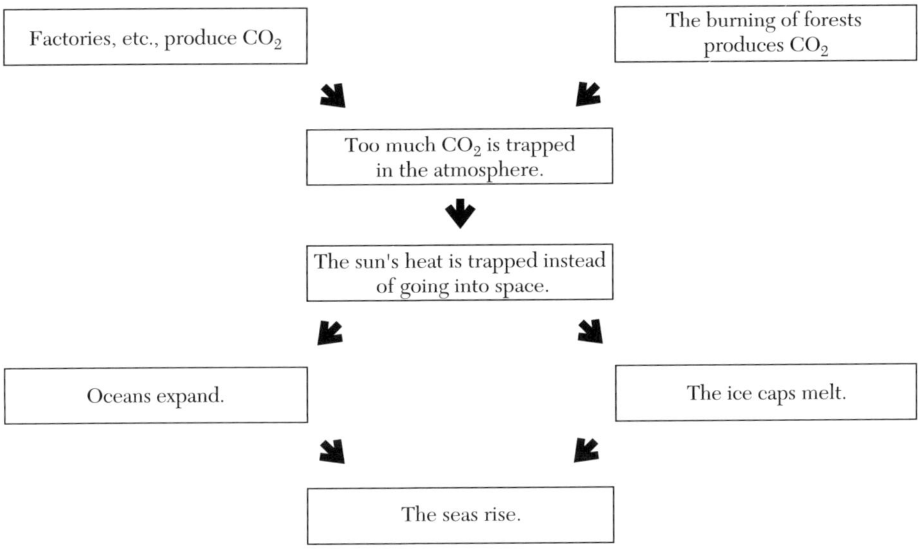

Task 5. This is an open-ended question, but students should have mentioned the following: flooding of low-lying areas, which are usually heavily populated and/or good agricultural land; changes in weather patterns resulting in changes in agriculture (i.e., more corn grown in Russia but less in the United States).

Task 6. Students will guess at cattle-ranchers or professional assassins hired by big companies. Some may know that, in fact, in 1990 Darli Alves da Silva and his son Darci, local cattle ranchers, were found guilty of Mendes' murder. His death is a warning in a symbolic sense: that there are very powerful vested interests which do not care about preserving rain forests and that ordinary people must therefore act together to save them.

Cleaner Cars for California

Prereading. If there are people in your class who don't have a car, try to pair them with people who do.

Task 1. 5, 2, 4, 6, 1, 3

Task 2. 1. c; 2. b; 3. b; 4. c

Task 4.

						1 T								
				2 S		O				3 U				
				M		X				R				
		4 C	H	O	K	I	N	G		B				
		R	■	G	■	N				A				
		5 U	N	S	U	S	T	A	I	N	A	B	L	E
		S								S				
6 P	H	A	S	E	O	U	T			P				
		D								R				
		E								A				
										W				
										L				

Task 5. Catalytic converters do not make exhaust gases 100% safe; some pollution still escapes. Changing to electric cars would simply move the problem further away, to areas downwind of the electricity generating plants. The causes may be similar, but the solutions being proposed are very different: public transport in Europe, "clean" cars in the United States. No they do not: they may own three cars each but presumably, like the other 62%, can only drive one at a time.

Task 6. The purpose here is to make students realize that the writer is biased: he does not mention hydrogen cars either because they are too experimental or because they would not cause air pollution. He seems to prefer the "European" solution: more and better public transport, town planning, etc.

Fluency Activities

Sharing World Knowledge.  = desertification; = deforestation; = air pollution; = radiation;  = toxic waste; = acid rain;  = ozone depletion. There are plenty of other threats to the environment, such as water pollution, fisheries depletion, species extinction, and global warming.

Matching. 1. d and i, possibly c; 2. e and i; 3. a, c, f, and i; 4. f and h, possibly g; 5. b and i; 6. g, possibly h. You may know of further possibilities.

Unit 7
Pride and Prejudice

Racial Equality at Work

Prereading

In small groups, find out if anyone has ever been refused a casual, part-time, or temporary job. What reasons might employers have for refusing to take on someone for such work?

Reading

Look at task 1 below and then read through the text quickly, without using a dictionary.

At half past twelve, Friday lunchtime, on 28 May, Errol Davidson walked up to a pub called the Corner Pin—just across the road from Wimbledon dog-racing stadium in south London. He didn't want a drink—he wanted a job, and that morning the Corner Pin had placed an ad in the local paper; they needed bar staff. Errol knew the job was still open because a friend had rung less then an hour before to check it out.

So into the lounge bar he walked and told the manager's wife he'd seen the ad. It was to be a brief exchange.

"Yes . . . no—it was seen to last night."

"It was seen to?"

"Yeah, so he's took somebody on, yes."

"So someone's on?"

"Yes, yes."

Out walked Errol, and then, one hour later, in walked Andy. Andy was the same age as Errol, had the same experience, and was similarly dressed. By this time the pub was noisy and busy with the lunchtime customers: the manager couldn't see Andy just now—could he come back tomorrow at eleven? So the job's still open? Yes.

The obvious punch line, of course, is that Errol is black and Andy is white. For Errol, the quite casual act of discrimination is almost banal; for most blacks it is an unremarkable fact of everyday life. But this time the discriminator has been caught in the act, because Errol and Andy are part of a team of jobless young people working on a week-long series of spot checks run by the Commission for Racial Equality.

When a copy of that conversation was presented to the Chef and Brewer company, who own the Corner Pin, they did their own checking. It was, they said, an "isolated and most regrettable incident."

But the CRE's spot check exercise showed how easily and regularly the law is broken by employers. One hundred jobs had been applied for: half had genuinely been filled, but in the remaining cases almost 60% of employers showed some discrimination against blacks, and, of those, 26% were quite obvious. A strong West Indian accent would often meet with the phone being slammed down at the other end.

Task 1

Which of these statements are true [T], which are false [F], and which are not answered in the text [NA]?

[ ] Errol and Andy are both rivals for the same job.
[ ] The pub manager's wife shows obvious discrimination against Errol.
[ ] The Chef and Brewer company were not speaking truthfully when they apologized for the incident.
[ ] This text shows that it is easy for blacks to prove when employers are discriminating against them.
[ ] Errol and Andy are working together to expose incidents of racial discrimination.

Task 2

Match these words and phrases from the text with the explanations.

exchange	too common and unremarkable to be noticed
punch line	found doing something wrong
banal	a quick, unannounced investigation
caught in the act	conversation
spot check	explanation of the story
isolated	happening only once

Extract from David Henshaw, "Racial Equality at Work," *Listener,* 1 July 1982.

Task 3

Look at the five-line exchange in paragraph 2. It is in very colloquial British English. Try to rewrite it so that it is easier to understand.

Task 4

How would you have felt, if you had been one of the following people?

a. Errol, when the manager's wife lied to him?
b. Andy, when he was offered a job interview? Why?
c. the manager, when he realized he'd been caught in the act of discrimination?

Note down a few words to describe how you would have felt, and compare them with your neighbors.

a.

b.

c.

Task 5

In paragraph 6 the text says "60% of employers showed some discrimination against blacks." What does this mean? In what ways might the employers have shown some discrimination? In groups, think of examples and write them down.

Asians in Australia

Prereading

a. What words do you associate with Australia? Try to think of nine different words, each containing one of the letters in AUSTRALIA.

A
U
S
T
R
A
L
I
A

b. You are going to read a text about immigration to Australia. What do you expect the mood of the text will be (e.g., optimistic, negative)? Why?

Reading

Look at task 1 below and then read through the text quickly, without using a dictionary.

When, in 1976, a wooden fishing boat, the *Kien Gang,* dropped anchor off a suburb of Darwin, for many people an Australia imagined only in fear and caricature was inaugurated. "A country whose immigration policy was built on the rock of Asian exclusion was to take in large numbers of Asians. . . ." In the years since the end of the Vietnam War Australia has given refuge to more people from Indochina than any country except the United States. In the late 1980s almost half of all newcomers to Australia were from Asia. Almost half the schoolchildren have at least one parent born in another country and a third of the populations of the two principal cities were born outside Australia.

In 1986 the Department of Immigration and Ethnic Affairs published the results of one of the most comprehensive surveys of attitudes among Australians and Asians living side by side. The great majority of Australians interviewed expressed positive views about their Asian neighbors, whom they no longer regarded in terms of preconceived stereotypes. There was no evidence of "ghetto formation" among Asians, a majority of whom reported that they "had an Australian neighbor whom they regarded as a casual friend." In Sydney's far western suburb of Cabramatta, the Cousins and the Kooks speak little of each other's language, but together they celebrate Chinese New Year and exchange Christmas gifts. Leila Cousins, who looks out for the Kooks' children when the Kooks are at work, said, "We have been here since the 1940s and we have seen **them all:** the British, the Italians, and now the Vietnamese. I think it makes our life interesting."

This understanding of cultural differences is part of an attitude and a commitment that I have found reflected widely. **It** is in the best Australian newspapers, which both celebrate "multiculturalism" and provide examples of harmony among "old" and "new" Australians. The headlines say "Across the Culture Gap to be Best of Neighbors and Friends" and "Harmony on the Street Where the Races Meet," and the stories report the common ground between people. It is in many of the multiracial schools, which foster pride in ethnic background rather than a denial of **it;** it is in the energy of teachers and specialists committed to breaking down stereotypes; and it is in many innovative and often poorly funded teaching aid programs. This "reaching out" by a substantial group of "old" Australians is reciprocated in the constant celebration of diversity by immigrants themselves: in the carnivals and festivals and impromptu events that are now part of the quality and confidence of Australian street life. On a Saturday morning in the west of Sydney, a traditional Lao wedding procession makes its way through the streets where, less than a generation past, **you** were careful not to speak your language, let alone sing and laugh in it.

Racism does, of course, still exist. Many are prevented from using their skills; for instance, the best Australia can offer an architectural draftsperson from Chile, Peter Llana, is work as a ditchdigger and cleaner. Australian professional groups remain Anglocentric, tradition bound, and discriminatory. The test given to immigrant doctors is said to be so hard that recently graduated Australian doctors would not be able to pass it.

In 1988 an official inquiry into immigration proposed that only a naturalized citizen should have welfare rights. **The measures** would emulate Britain and divide immigrants into citizens and noncitizens. These noncitizens would not be able to vote and would be excluded from welfare benefits; neither would their children have an automatic right to citizenship.

There is still racism, deep and historic, but in everyday life the worst, perhaps, is indifference. One explanation **for this** is the consensus of support for immigration that has spanned the political landscape. Two generations of Australians have been educated to understand that immigration is "good" for everybody—gastronomically, culturally, and politically.

Task 1

Which of the following are the main points of the text [M] and which are supplementary material [S]?

[ ] Australian newspapers have played an important role in promoting racial harmony and multiculturalism.
[ ] The key elements of multiculturalism are respecting cultural differences while living together in racial harmony.
[ ] Australia's immigration policy toward Asians has changed dramatically since 1976.
[ ] Racism still exists in official and professional circles.
[ ] Dividing immigrants into citizens and noncitizens would be a step backward for Australia's multicultural policy.
[ ] The success of Australia's attempt to build a multicultural society is evident in people's attitudes, in education, in the media, and in many other areas.

Task 2

Think of questions to which the following statements are the answers.

It showed that in general "old" Australians and Asians were good neighbors.
They "reach out" to them.
by holding carnivals and traditional festivals
because he can't get work as an architectural draftsperson

Adapted from John Pilger, *A Secret Country* (New York: Alfred A. Knopf, 1988), 119–26.

Task 3

Look at the words and phrases printed in bold in the text and decide what they refer to.

them all (who?)
it (what?)
it (what?)
you (who?)
the measures (what measures?)
for this (for what?)

Task 4

a. Complete the following sentences by putting one word from the text into each of the blanks. The letters of the three words are jumbled in the diamond.

I
TGL
HEAT
FUTURED
GRAN
OEZ
E

1. A ____________ is a part of a city where many people of a particular race or nationality live, excluded from the main stream of society.
2. If someone is ____________ they become a citizen of a country they were not born in.
3. If someone gives you ____________, they give you somewhere safe to escape to.

b. Now do the same for the following three sentences.

C
SIN
EFYT
EVERI
TINTIE
DORFS
PYRE
DES
E

1. ___________ are fixed general images of particular groups of people. They are often exaggerated or inaccurate.
2. The immigrants have great ___________ because each group has its own traditions, living styles, and customs.
3. ___________ is a complete lack of interest in someone/something.

Task 5

Make six sentences by matching the subjects in column A with the rest of the sentences in column B.

A	B
In 1976 many people in Australia	had equal voting and welfare rights.
By the mid-80s most Australians	made up one-third of the population of Australia's two main cities
By the mid-80s immigrants	often faced discrimination in the job market.
Good Australian newspapers	seemed to get along well with their Asian neighbors.
Well-qualified immigrants	feared Asian immigration.
At the time of writing, all immigrants	encourage positive attitudes toward multiculturalism.

Task 6

Choose the question that applies to you and discuss it in small groups.

a. If you are an immigrant, how is the situation described in the text different from your own situation?
b. If you are not an immigrant, does this text make you want to emigrate to Australia or does it put you off?

Fluency Activities

Evaluation

What is a "minority group"? Look at the statements that follow and choose the ones that define a "minority group."

a. They have a different skin color from the majority.
b. They came originally from a different country.
c. They have particular physical features.
d. They have particular cultural features.
e. They perceive themselves as distinct (separate) from the majority.
f. They usually receive unequal treatment in society.
g. They are less civilized than the majority.

Compare your choices with neighboring groups.

Sharing World Knowledge

Use your own and your classmates' knowledge to answer the following questions. In which countries would you find the following minorities?

Inuit	Kurds
Tamils	Irish

Which minorities would you find in these countries?

New Zealand	
Japan	
Your country	

Can you name any countries that have no minorities?

Information Sharing

What do you know about minorities in your own country?
How did they come to be there?
Do they suffer from discrimination? How?
What could be done to improve their situation?
In order to build a multicultural society, which institutions must play a major role?

Creative Thinking

The role of education is perhaps the most important in encouraging multiculturalism. How could multiculturalism be taught in schools? Think of three or four guiding principles for multicultural education.

Choose two subjects from the following list. How could you make the content of lessons in these subjects reflect your principles?

history	geography	literature	biology
math	music	economics	civics

Sharing Your Memories

Think about your own school career.

Did any teacher ever teach you to respect minorities? How?
Was your education prejudiced against minorities? If so, in what ways?

Project

Look through recent newspapers and magazines and collect articles, stories, advertisements, etc., that feature ethnic minorities. Which give positive images, which are negative, and which are aimed at the ethnic minority and which at the general public?

Debate

Divide yourselves into two teams (For and Against) and brainstorm as many arguments as you can. Then either split up your arguments among the team and each side take turns presenting and defending your case, or pair off with a member of the opposing team and argue it out face to face. Argue either for or against the following statement.

The contribution of ethnic and cultural minorities to our society is undervalued.

Teacher's Notes and Answer Key

Racial Equality at Work

Task 1. F (though they are *acting* as rivals for the job), NA (it depends whether you think the discrimination is obvious), NA (a matter of opinion), F, T

Task 2. exchange = conversation; *punch line* = explanation of the story; *banal* = too common and unremarkable to be noticed; *caught in the act* = found doing something wrong; *spot check* = a quick, unannounced investigation; *isolated* = happening only once

Task 3. A possible answer would be the following.

"Yes . . . No—the job vacancy was filled last night."
"It was dealt with?"
"Yes, he has employed someone, yes."
"So someone has been employed?"
"Yes, yes."

Asians in Australia

Task 1. S, M, S, S, S, M

Task 2. Suitable questions are as follows.

What was the general conclusion of the Department of Immigration and Ethnic Affairs (DIE) survey?
What is the attitude of most "old" Australians toward the Asian immigrants?
How do the Asian immigrants share their cultures with other Australians?
Why is Peter Llana working as a ditchdigger and cleaner?

Of course there are many other possible questions that fit the answers.

Task 3. them all = immigrant groups who have moved into that area since the 1940s (British, Italians, and Vietnamese); *it* = understanding of cultural difference/commitment to multiculturalism; *it* = ethnic background; *you* = earlier immigrants; *the measures* = the proposals that only naturalized citizens should get welfare rights; *for this* = for the general lack of racism in everyday life

Task 4. a. 1. ghetto; 2. naturalized; 3. refuge. b. 1. stereotypes; 2. diversity; 3. indifference.

Task 5. In 1976 many people in Australia feared Asian immigration.

By the mid-80s most Australians seemed to get along well with their Asian neighbors.
By the mid-80s immigrants made up one-third of the population of Australia's two main cities.
Good Australian newspapers encourage positive attitudes toward multiculturalism.
Well-qualified immigrants often face discrimination in the job market.
At the time of writing all immigrants had equal voting and welfare rights.

Fluency Activities

Evaluation. d, e, and f constitute the most generally accepted definition. The activity is left purposely ambiguous to see whether there is any discussion of ethnic, religious, or sexual minorities. In statement d, if "culture" is interpreted in the broadest possible sense, it would encompass all such minorities. However, most of the activities presented here deal with *ethnic* minorities.

World Knowledge. Small numbers of many ethnic groups are found in most countries of the world (a point worth stressing), but there are large communities of these ethnic groups in the following countries: Inuit in Canada, Alaska, Russia, and Greenland; Kurds in Iraq, Turkey, Iran, and Syria; Tamils in Sri Lanka, India, and Singapore; Irish in Britain, the United States, Canada, Australia, and New Zealand.
New Zealand—Maori, recent immigrant groups from Europe, Asia, and Polynesia
Japan—Koreans, Chinese, Ainu, Southeast Asians, Burakumin (who are not racially or culturally different from the majority)
We cannot think of any countries that have no minorities, possibly Iceland?

Information Sharing. Most of the questions are open-ended. For the last question, make sure some students have mentioned (1) education, (2) the media, and (3) laws that prohibit discrimination and promote equal rights for all members of society.

Creative Thinking. The kinds of things that students should be noting down include raising awareness of, appreciation, and respect for other cultures. If students are given enough time to come to grips with the topic they may well come up with a surprising variety of specific ideas for each chosen discipline.

Project. This activity could be exploited further by encouraging individuals or pairs of students to choose a specific ethnic minority and prepare a wall poster or presentation about that ethnic group's way of life and place in the community.

Unit 8
Out of Our Minds

Bored Out of Life

Prereading

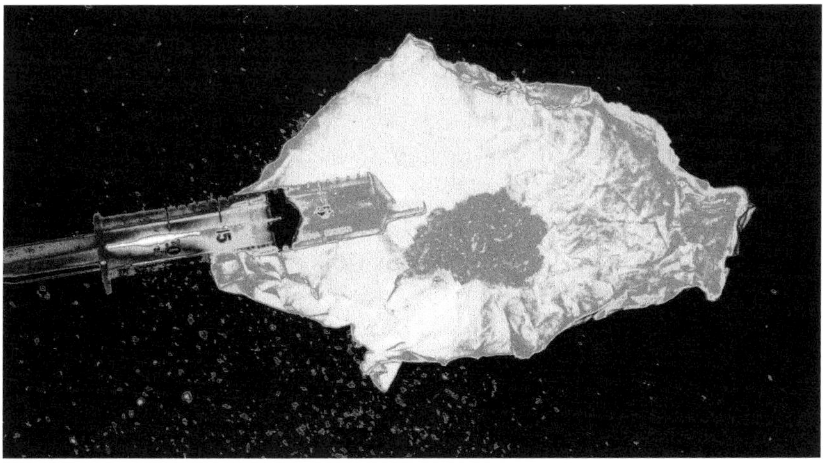

What words does this photograph suggest to you? In groups, make a list of your ideas.

Reading

Look at task 1 below and then read through the text quickly, without using a dictionary.

Back in the sixties I had a problem: my husband enjoyed lovemaking rather more than I did. He complained that he wasn't getting enough. Believing that all problems had a practical solution, I decided to go to a specialist clinic for help. The young male doctor listened to me and then reached for his prescription pad. "I have just the thing," he cried with delight. "It'll make you feel much sexier. It's called Valium!" It made me feel very pleasant, relaxed, and stress-free, but it didn't make me any sexier; in fact, one of the side effects of tranquilizers is to suppress the sex drive. I stopped taking the pills after a while. The enjoyable sensation had disappeared, and there didn't seem much point in continuing. I was, however, left with the firm belief that mood-altering drugs were a good thing.

My fragile marriage broke up, and I was left a single parent; somehow I coped, and without drugs. Then I broke my leg. My doctor began writing prescriptions for painkillers, DF 118, a powerful drug very similar to morphine, and also for sleeping pills, first barbiturates and then another wonder drug, Mandrax, one of the most abused drugs on the market. In 1978 it was withdrawn because of its dangerous potential; my pusher, the doctor, simply replaced it with one of the newer drugs available. And he gave me lots and lots of my old friend Valium to fight the boredom and the pressures.

For years, I poured pills down my throat and was legally stoned for 24 hours each day. Never once did any doctor who wrote these prescriptions talk to me about the danger I was in. I lied to myself more and more. "Me addicted? Nonsense. Valium isn't addictive. Sleeping pills, painkillers—I can give them up any time." I never listened to the voice in my head that whispered: "You don't need drugs to get through life."

Slowly and surely I was destroying myself and causing great pain to those who loved me. Drugged people do remarkably little constructive work, least of all on their own lives. I lost all self-confidence and felt hopeless. Eventually, when I was near to the breaking point, a sharp young doctor told me: "You need help, not pills."

Withdrawal from the opium-based painkillers was nasty but short and exactly like a description of heroin withdrawal: vomiting, cramps, and muscle pain for three weeks. Sleeping pill withdrawal lasts longer, and the major symptoms are insomnia and tension. Yet it was getting off the tranquilizers that was the real killer. The withdrawal takes forever and includes miseries as diverse as anxiety attacks and incontinence. It took five years for me to be drug free, but I did it and I'm very proud of myself. Even now, three years since I last took a Valium, I still have bad days . . . days when my nerves jangle and my body aches as it adjusts to life without drugs.

For seventeen years I lived in a gray world of defeat and numbed despair, without pain. But our troubles are our finest teachers and without them, and without pain, there is no growth. I feel fear, anxiety, anger, and grief now; all the feelings I blocked for so many years. I experience and accept them. Life buzzes with color and excitement. No longer doped, I choose my life.

Adapted from an article by Susie Pritchard in the *Guardian*, September 1989.

Task 1

Look at these four statements. In each case, all the answers are true, but which of the three choices gives the main point of the text?

1. She couldn't give up the drugs for many years because
   a. She couldn't admit she was addicted.
   b. The drugs are addictive.
   c. Her doctors encouraged her to take them.
2. The drugs she took were
   a. legal but abused
   b. unnecessary
   c. similar to, and as harmful as, many illegal drugs
3. The drugs destroyed her by
   a. breaking up her marriage
   b. suppressing her normal human emotions
   c. poisoning her body
4. She began taking drugs
   a. because at first they were necessary
   b. on her doctor's advice
   c. because she didn't realize they were dangerous

Task 2

Complete this crossword puzzle by using words from the text.

Down

1. unable to think clearly because of drugs
2. process of giving up a drug to which you were addicted
3. needing a drug so much that you have to take it
5. someone who provides an addict with drugs

Across

4. heavily affected by drugs
6. used in a wrong way
7. changing your emotional state (two words, hyphenated)

Task 3

Complete this chart, listing the names of the drugs she took and the withdrawal symptoms she suffered when she gave them up.

	Names of Drugs	Withdrawal Symptoms
Painkillers		
Sleeping pills		
Tranquilizers		

Task 4

Which of these statements are true [T] and which are false [F]?

[ ] The doctor first prescribed Valium to increase her sex drive.
[ ] Valium was necessary to fight the pain of her broken leg.
[ ] Mandrax was banned because it was more dangerous than other prescription drugs.
[ ] She lost interest in life because she was addicted to drugs.
[ ] It took her five years to give up all the drugs.
[ ] Even now she still suffers from occasional withdrawal symptoms.

Task 5

What possible reasons could her doctors have had for continually giving the writer drugs? Make a list of all the ideas you can think of.

____

____

____

____

____

____

____

____

World Evil with Its Roots in the North-South Divide

Prereading

a. Look at the title. Can you guess what the text is about?

b. Look at the map. Which countries are shaded in dark gray and why? Which countries are shaded in light gray and why?

c. Where are (i) tobacco and (ii) cannabis (also called marijuana and hashish) grown? Mark the areas where you think they are grown on the map.

Reading and Prediction

Read through the text section by section. Try to answer the questions at the end of each section *before* reading the next section.

The **expansionist** countries of Europe and, later, the United States, used their industrial power to produce and trade in tobacco, alcohol, opium, hashish, and cocaine on a world scale. It was Britain, supported by France, that imposed by force the free trade of opium in China, where it was not widely used. Within 50 years, thousands of tonnes of opium contributed to the **disintegration** of one of the most populous and most civilized countries in the world. Queen Victoria turned a deaf ear to the requests of the Chinese emperor, who had banned the import and consumption of opium. She felt that it would be **inopportune** to give up such a major source of **revenue.** Her government **provoked** two opium wars, in 1839 and 1856, and seized Hong Kong. Thus the first drug wars were waged and won by the biggest **trafficker** of recent history—the British crown—and not by some **narcodollar baron.**

In the twentieth century, some drugs were classified as "legal" and others as "illegal." Which? How are they similar, and how are the two groups different?

From then on, **narcotics** became a key element of world trade, but the rules of that trade were not fixed until the major powers, from 1912, imposed their views on the community of nations. In classifying the **substances** that are addictive, damage the health, and create social problems, a distinction is made between legal drugs (chiefly tobacco, alcohol, and medical products) and illegal drugs (over 150 natural and **synthetic** substances), which are totally **banned.**

On one side, then, are the so-called good drugs, which are manufactured in the North by the leading industrialized countries, and on the other there are the "bad drugs" produced by the Third World. "Good drugs" are in the hands of powerful tobacco, alcohol, and pharmaceuticals multinationals, which quite lawfully **swamp** the markets of North and South with their products. They have a direct interest in ensuring the disappearance of "bad drugs"—despite the fact that their own drugs cause far greater **ravages.**

In France (population 55 million) how many people die every year as a result of

a.	tobacco?	Is it:	600	6,000	60,000?
b.	alcohol?	Is it:	350	3,500	35,000?
c.	all illegal drugs?	Is it:	200	2,000	20,000?

In France, tobacco is the direct cause of 60,000 deaths a year and alcohol 35,000, while the consumption of legal psychoactive drugs such as barbiturates has gone up five times since 1976. Illegal drugs cause less than 200 deaths a year in France. In the United States, the really big health problem facing teenagers is not **crack,** but alcoholism.

The most common illegal drugs are derived from plants such as poppies, coca, and cannabis, all of which are cultivated chiefly on poor soil in remote regions of **destitute** Third World countries. When the farmers sell their crops, they get very little return: their income represents one-thousandth of the total world heroin and cocaine market.

So why do farmers grow illegal drugs rather than other cash crops?

Even so, this is still more than they will get if they grow their traditional cash crops. For example, in the United States, the price of cocaine has almost doubled since President Bush announced his "drug war" campaign, and the price of coffee has collapsed. One country, Colombia, exports large quantities of both commodities, which provide most of its export earnings. The market has simply chosen between the two; the growers have been encouraged to switch from coffee to coca.

This also highlights the **duplicity** of Western countries and above all the United States, the world's biggest importer of coffee as well as cocaine. Washington made no effort to renew the international coffee agreement which **expired** in July 1989, thus leading to the collapse in world coffee prices. In fact, the United States deliberately **sabotaged** the agreement with the aim of paying a little less for a commodity produced on a massive scale by destitute and **debt-ridden** Latin American countries.

The coffee crisis was passed over in silence by the leading industrialized countries. Plenty of brash publicity surrounded Bush's promise to give the Colombian government $65 million of aid to fight the drug barons. Yet, if it is to make up for the foreign currency losses it has incurred in the coffee sector, Colombia will have to rely more than ever on the $4 billion "earned" by the local drug barons.

It is difficult to see why the Americans are focusing such attention on the Andean area and on cocaine, which accounts for less than a quarter of total drug sales in the United States: $20 billion out of $88 billion (compared with $40 billion for cannabis and $28 billion for opiates).

Can you think of any other reason why money from growing drugs is necessary in certain parts of the world? (The map at the start of this reading may give you an idea.)

While cocaine production doubled between 1984 and 1988, the same was true of other narcotics: the output of opium poppies increased eight times in Laos and doubled in Burma. Another reason for the huge increase in drug production over the past five years is the need to finance local **conflicts,** for example in Afghanistan and in Lebanon, where the various warring parties pay for their weapons with the **proceeds** of the heroin they sell to organized crime.

Task 1

Which of the following would provide the best conclusion to the text?

a. It is clear that drugs have been an important part of world trade for a long time. Therefore, would it not be more sensible to legalize illegal drugs, so as to give the South a fair share of the trade and to allow more effective international control of terrorism?

b. The only way production of illegal drugs can be reduced is through the resolution of regional conflicts and a reform of the currently unfair terms of trade between the countries of the North and the South.

c. Combating the destructive effects of illegal drugs—the sacrifice of young lives in the North and the impoverishment of farmers in the South—will require both vast amounts of money from Western governments and extensive education campaigns worldwide.

Task 2

Mark the order, from [1] to [6], in which the following ideas appear in the text.

[ ] Legal drugs cause more harm worldwide than illegal ones.

[ ] The industrial powers fixed the rules as to what are legal and what are illegal drugs.

[ ] The earliest drug traffickers were European traders supported by their governments.

[ ] The sale of drugs provides the money and weapons that are needed to wage local wars.

[ ] Third world farmers get a very small proportion of the street price of illegal drugs.

[ ] The United States has helped to destroy cash crop markets, thus encouraging farmers to switch to growing illegal drugs.

Adapted from an article by Christian de Brie, *Le Monde Diplomatique*, October 1989, translated and reprinted in the *Guardian Weekly* 141, no. 20 (19 November 1989): 14 and 16.

Task 3

Look at the words in **bold** in the text. Circle the ones that you don't know. Which of the words that you do not know prevent you from understanding something important in the text? Find out what they mean, preferably without using a dictionary.

Task 4

List the facts presented in this text that are new to you. Did any of these facts particularly surprise you? In groups, compare and discuss your lists.

____

____

____

____

____

____

____

____

Fluency Activities

Sharing World Knowledge

Look at the list of drugs in the chart below. Which of the following statements apply to which drugs? Check [√] the appropriate boxes.

a. illegal
b. legal on prescription only
c. legal and easily available
d. addictive
e. causes chronic disease
f. causes violent crime
g. overdose can kill

	a	b	c	d	e	f	g
tobacco			√	√	√		
crack							
Valium							
morphine							
glue							
marijuana							
alcohol							
heroin							

What do your answers tell you about the connection between a drug's legality and how dangerous it is?

Opinion Survey

Ask your partner the following questions and note down her/his answers in the boxes.

	Strongly Agree	Tend to Agree	Tend to Disagree	Stongly Disagree
Patients with smoking-related diseases should pay for their own medical care.				
People caught drunk-driving should be banned from driving for life.				
Smoking marijuana at home should be legalized.				
People caught selling hard drugs should be sentenced to life imprisonment.				
Governments should raise taxes on alcohol and tobacco to cover the costs of drinkers' and smokers' health care.				
Governments should ban the sale of tobacco.				
Governments should ban the sale of alcohol.				
Governments should allow hard drug addicts to get their drugs on prescription.				
The sale of glue and thinner should be banned to people under 25.				
Doctors should be required to tell patients about the addictiveness of the drugs they prescribe.				

Which statements produced the greatest consensus of opinion? Which produced the least consensus?

Brainstorm and Evaluation

What could you do if you found out that your best friend had started using crack? List as many ideas as possible even if they seem crazy.

Exchange your list with another group. Which of their ideas do you like best? Why?

Personal Questions

If you were trying to find out about other people's smoking habits or drinking habits, what questions would you ask them? Choose EITHER smoking OR drinking and note down at least ten questions.

Exchange your questions with someone in another group. Look at her/his questions and answer only those questions that you want to answer.

Creative Dictation

Your teacher is going to dictate a story to you about a convicted criminal. After writing the first sentence, decide on a suitable punishment and note it down. After writing each subsequent sentence, you may change the punishment if you wish.

	Punishment
1.	
2.	
3.	
4.	
5.	
6.	
7.	

Compare your dictations and discuss any important differences. Have you learned anything from this exercise?

Project

Collect information about drug use and abuse from newspapers, magazines, and television. Bring the information and share it with your classmates. What is the media's attitude toward drugs?

Debate

Divide yourselves into two teams (For and Against) and brainstorm as many arguments as you can. Then either split up your arguments among the team and each side take turns presenting and defending your case, or pair off with a member of the opposing team and argue it out face to face. Argue either for or against the following statement.

Smoking should be banned in all workplaces and all public places, including outdoors.

Teacher's Notes and Answer Key

Bored Out of Life

Task 1. 1. a; 2. c; 3. b; 4. b or c

Task 2.

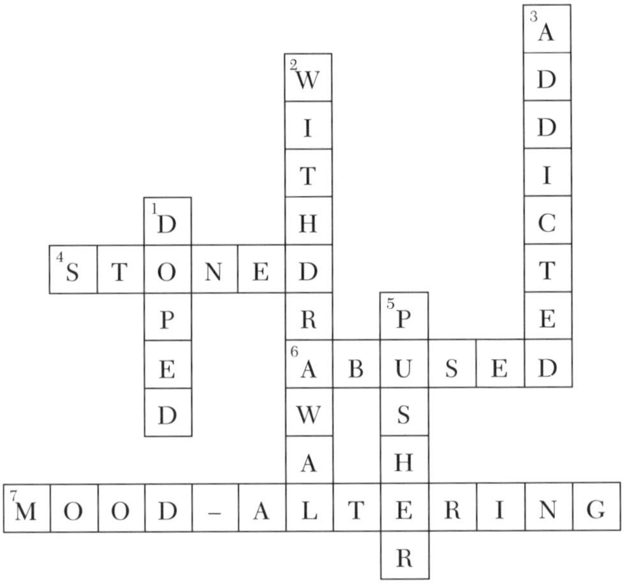

Task 3. Painkillers—DF118—vomiting, cramps, muscle pain; *sleeping pills*—barbiturates and Mandrax—insomnia, tension; *tranquilizers*—Valium—anxiety attacks, incontinence

Task 4. T, F, F, T, T, T

World Evil with Its Roots in the North-South Divide

Prereading. a. World evil refers to narcotics, and the article talks about them in terms of the rich and poorer countries of the world. b. Mexico, Colombia, Ecuador, Peru, Bolivia, and Brazil are the countries where coca leaves are grown (Colombia has been the center of cocaine production in recent years); Iran, Afghanistan, Pakistan, Burma

[Myanmar], Thailand, and Laos are the countries where opium poppies are grown (the Golden Triangle of Burma [Myanmar], Thailand, and Laos has been the center of heroin production in recent years). c. Tobacco is grown in many parts of the world including the United States, Cuba, southern Europe, the Middle East, the southern states of the Russian Federation, China, and the Philippines. Cannabis can also be grown in many parts of the world, including the Himalayan foothills, the United States, Mexico, North Africa, and the Middle East.

Reading and Prediction. In this text, there are prediction questions at the end of every section. Make sure that students predict answers to these questions before reading on. The subsequent section provides the answers.

Task 1. We think that the best answer is b.

Task 2. 3, 2, 1, 6, 4, 5

Fluency Activities

Sharing World Knowledge. It is difficult to be precise about this since legal restrictions vary from country to country and medical knowledge is incomplete, but the following seemed to be the norm in most Western countries in 1996. *Tobacco:* c, d, and e; *crack:* a, d, f, and g; *Valium:* b (depending upon where you live), d and g; *morphine:* b, d, and g?; *glue:* c, d, and e?; *marijuana:* a (depending upon where you live) and d?; *alcohol:* c, d?, e, f?, and g; *heroin:* a, d, e?, f, and g

Creative Dictation. Dictate the following, sentence by sentence.

1. Someone has been convicted of selling crack.
2. to teenagers
3. The seller is black.
4. She is a single parent with four young children.
5. She has AIDS but cannot afford medical treatment.
6. She is an addict herself.
7. This is her third offense.

Unit 9
Dead End Street

Inside a Third World City

Prereading

Have you ever been to the capital of a Third World country or seen television programs about one? Make a list of 10–15 words or phrases that you would expect to appear in a description of such a city and its inhabitants.

____

____

____

____

Now read the text. Which of your words or their synonyms appear in the text?

Reading

Look at task 1 below and then read through the text quickly, without using a dictionary.

Steel and dark-glass skyscrapers rise around the expressways and landscaped gardens of the Parque de la Independencia, while half a mile away shanties built of wood and cardboard are crowded together down the steep hills that surround the city. Rich Bogota has managed to keep the homes of the poor out of sight, but the starving people will not hide away while the rich feast. They invade the center in their rags and dirt. Beggars line the pavements under the elegant shops of Avenida Jimenez and Carrera 7. A red-faced woman coughs and points to the baby asleep on her shoulder and holds out her hand for money—demanding, desperate. A cripple draws sidewalk pictures to collect money to pay for an operation. A starving man in his fifties, in a brown poncho that is far too big for him, plays a guitar while his ten-year old daughter scrapes a plastic pipe with a knife and her baby sister shakes a maraca. Their happy music is not reflected in the deep misery of the father's face or the girls' hungry anxiety. Then there are the rubbish people, almost as ragged and dirty as the trash they collect from the city's waste bins. Women carrying huge piles of cardboard on their backs and dirty-faced boys pushing ramshackle carts full of trash mix with stylish secretaries and well-dressed bank employees. They wander the smart suburbs, collecting rubbish before the city dustcart comes around, and the uncaring rich—rich enough to afford $20 for a full bottle of whisky—are so unbelievably shameless that they make the boys pay for the empty bottles.

The rich created this problem: the lawyers and businesspeople who own huge estates in the country and pay their peasants so little that they have to leave for the cities; the landlords who build city slums without light, roads, or water and charge terrible rents to live in them. The rich brought the poor here and kept them poor once they got here. Perhaps it is only right that they should not be allowed to feel comfortable in their wealth. The *gamines* (young street thieves) are at the front of this great army of the poor. They jump onto buses and sing tragic songs for money. They beg, sad-faced and hands held out, dirtying clean suits with their grubby hands. Above all they rob, mug, and terrorize the middle classes, taking from them the possessions they have bought with the profit squeezed out of the poor.

Task 1

Which of the following is the main idea of the text?

a. The poor cause a lot of problems in Bogota.
b. It's better to be rich than poor in Bogota.
c. The poverty in Bogota is the fault of the rich.
d. Bogota is a city of great contrasts.

Task 2

What is the writer's attitude toward the poor people?

a. neutral and factual
b. patronizing
c. sympathetic
d. a little critical

Adapted from Paul Harrison, *Inside the Third World*, 3d ed. (Harmondsworth: Penguin, 1993), 153–54.

Task 3

Match the words from the text with the definitions.

shanties	badly made and in need of repair
rags	someone who cannot walk
cripple	small, badly built houses
ramshackle	rob with violence
shameless	old, worn-out clothes
mug	with no concern for one's bad behavior

Task 4

Which phrases tell you the following facts?

There is no free medical care here. (para. 1)

The rich have no sympathy for the poor. (para. 1)

The city's poor came from the countryside. (para. 2)

There is a lot of crime in the city. (para. 2)

Task 5

In what ways do you think the lives of the rich are different from the poor in this city? Use the text to get as much information as you can and then add your own ideas. Make notes about these points.

Rich Colombians		Poor Colombians
	Homes	
	Jobs	
	Food and Drink	
	Schooling	
	Health Care	
	Other Things	

Task 6

Paragraph 2 says that the rich "kept them poor once they got here." Try to imagine how they do this, discuss with your group, and make a list of your ideas.

What could be done to improve the future of the poor people of Bogota? Again, brainstorm, discuss, and list your ideas.

Inside an English City

Prereading

How many people are unemployed in the district where you live? In groups, make a list of the problems that you associate with unemployment. Then compare your list with your classmates'.

Reading

The text tells us about the lives of unemployed teenagers living in Sunderland, a city in Northeast England that used to be a major industrial center, but that has suffered from high unemployment since the 1970s.
Look at task 1 below and then read through the text quickly, without using a dictionary.

A group of boys, seventeen and eighteen. Zit, Tim, Scruff. A skinhead with a red T-shirt, jeans, and Dr. Marten boots is known as Knobhead because his short hair emphasizes the shape of his forehead. The boy with dark hair is called Zit because he has spots on his face, and Scruff has big safety pins holding his tattered suede jacket together; he wears rain boots and mud-splashed trousers. They live on Pennywell estate, a vast spreading estate in the northwest of Sunderland, a piece of plain concrete geometry, housing so many people whose redundancy stares them in the face from their earliest years—people whose lives are no longer shaped by coal mine or shipyard or factory but simply by the monstrous images of material wealth that are thrust at them from the moment they are born, which seem to taunt and laugh at them more and more as they grow up. Their poverty seems to increase as the power and the wealth of the rich grow, power and wealth that no longer even seem to have been achieved at the expense of their labor but, mysteriously, at the expense of their enforced idleness and lack of resources.

Their lives depend on money that will buy them excitement, or escape. Without money, they have to make do with the most unsatisfying experiences: quick sex in some girl's front room while her Mam's out shopping; sleep until midday in the grubby, unchanged sheets, with the faded pictures of yesterday's heroes on the bedroom wall and the litter of broken toys in the boxes under the bed; the ride in the car stolen from behind the barbed wire under Genevieve's disco on Saturday night; drinking from the bottles of beer taken from the workingmen's club; buying new clothes with the money taken from a woman's shopping basket in the supermarket downtown.

The high spirits and energy of these young people are lost in their aimless fantasies that grow in the space that has developed in their heads from their wasted sense of purpose. They are full of boasts and sarcasm, a hard skin hiding the sense of being unwanted, that the society in which they have grown up despises and humiliates them. "When you don't have anything to do, you sit in the house all day, gamble on the horses, watch television, wait for time to pass. You feel like killing yourself; perhaps somebody'd notice you then." The references to suicide are frequent among the young unemployed. They are not serious threats for the most part but another way of expressing the feeling of lack of worth. This sense of hopelessness cannot express itself against the brilliant consumer spectacle, so it turns inward and destroys their self esteem, then reemerges as a desperate kind of violence, or racism.

Their conversation wanders; they talk of things they've stolen and tell one another funny, bawdy stories. They talk about what happens to you when you die: whether you go into other forms, other bodies, what you feel when you are dying. But they soon become locked into images of violence and horror from TV and films, and the day to day realities of their lives become mixed up with images of man-made robots, journeys into space, beings from other worlds. All the searching and questioning, their concern with human mortality, are diverted into channels that are making money for others. And it hurts to see their captivity, the new subordination that has found other ways than hunger and hard work to keep them in their place.

Task 1

Match these paragraph summaries to the four paragraphs in the text.

[ ] Their feelings of rejection and uselessness lead to frustration, talk of suicide, and even violence.

[ ] When they aren't sleeping, they spend their time in search of cheap, and often illegal, thrills.

[ ] Their curiosity about the world is controlled by images that are created by moneymakers.

[ ] Because they are growing up in an area of industrial decay, they can look forward neither to work nor money but are surrounded by images of wealth.

Task 2

Think of questions to which these are the answers.

They refer to the boys' appearance.
mining, shipbuilding, and manufacturing industry
Their self-esteem is destroyed.
by having quick sex, sleeping, and stealing things
Sometimes they tell funny stories, but at other times their conversation is very profound.
violence, horror, and science fiction

Adapted from Jeremy Seabrook, *Unemployment* (London: Quartet Books, 1982).

Task 3

The following words all appear in the text; they are connected with either (a) hopelessness, (b) threatening behavior, or (c) control. Decide which words are connected with which concept.

thrust at	taunt	enforced
locked into	aimless	despises
unwanted	humiliates	subordination
wasted	destroys	captivity
unsatisfying	lack of worth	keep in place

What is the effect of using so many words like these in the text?

Task 4

Which of these statements does the writer believe to be true?

a. Teenagers who face long-term unemployment in their hometowns should move away so that they can get work and money and so enjoy all the things they see advertised on TV.

b. Teenagers who can't find work soon engage in antisocial and criminal behavior and become obsessed with violence and death.

c. The sense of hopelessness of unemployed teenagers is made worse when they live in a society whose values are dominated by the urge to make and spend money.

d. Unemployment among teenagers is one of the major causes of crime, antisocial behavior, and thoughts of suicide.

e. If unemployed teenagers watched less television, they wouldn't be so violent and suicidal.

Task 5

Which of these statements from the text are facts [F] and which are the writer's opinions [O]?

[ ] Without money they have to make do with the most unsatisfactory experiences.

[ ] They are full of boasts and sarcasm.

[ ] The references to suicide are frequent among the young unemployed.

[ ] Their poverty seems to increase as the power and wealth of the rich grow.

[ ] People's lives in Sunderland are no longer shaped by coal mine, shipyard, or factory.

[ ] Their lives are shaped by the monstrous images of material wealth that are thrust at them.

Task 6

What questions would you like to ask Zit, Tim, Scruff, and Knobhead about their lives?

Task 7

How could the lives of these teenagers be improved? List all the ways you can think of.

Fluency Activities

Information Gap

Think again about the situations described in the two texts. In what ways are the young people's lives in Bogota and Sunderland similar, and in what ways are they different? Note down three similarities and three differences.

	Similarities	Differences
1.		
2.		
3.		

Think about the poor people in your country. Is their poverty more like that in Bogota, or Sunderland, or is it different from both?

Evaluation 1

Go through the following list quickly and check [√] the items that you consider to be signs of poverty.

- ☐ not having a Walkman
- ☐ having only one pair of shoes
- ☐ children having to share a bed
- ☐ no electricity in your home
- ☐ relying on a social security check
- ☐ eating meat or fish only once a week
- ☐ being pregnant again
- ☐ having only a black-and-white TV
- ☐ leaving school as soon as the law allows
- ☐ wearing hand-me-down clothes
- ☐ being illiterate
- ☐ only having a night out once a month
- ☐ sending your preteen children out to work
- ☐ fresh fruit a luxury
- ☐ not having hot running water in your home
- ☐ not expecting to live beyond 50
- ☐ less than two meals a day

Compare your judgments with your partner(s) and explain them where there are differences. When you checked these items were you thinking about your own country, the developed world, the Third World, or all of these places?

Evaluation 2

What causes poverty in the Third World? Decide which of the following are the MAIN causes.

having too many children
war
lack of jobs
decline of traditional community structure
droughts and floods
lack of goods to sell
a lazy attitude toward work
how land is distributed
other (please specify) ________________________________

Compare and discuss your choices in small groups.

Guesstimates

Use your world knowledge to complete the following chart by inserting these figures: 10%, 15%, 20%, 20%, 65%, 70%. Compare your chart with your partner(s). Do you agree?

	% of World Population	% of World Income
Rich capitalist countries		
Ex-Soviet-bloc countries		
Third World countries		

Creative Thinking

All of the statements below are true. Construct an explanation that includes all the elements to show how they are connected with world poverty.

"Every minute of every day 30 people in the world die because of hunger or hunger-related diseases." (*Hungry for Change* [Oxford: Oxfam, 1986])

"Every minute of every day the EC destroys 2,130 kilos of fruit." (*Hungry for Change* [Oxford: Oxfam, 1986])

"In 1988, military spending in poor countries totalled $145 billion, enough to end absolute poverty within the next ten years." (Ben Jackson, *Poverty and the Planet* [Harmondsworth: Penguin, 1990], 174)

"El Salvador's peasant majority are crowded on to the poorest land because 2% of the people—known as the 'Fourteen Families'—control 60% of the land. (ibid., 155)

"It takes 16 kilos of grain to make 1 kilo of beef." (Susan George, *How the Other Half Dies* [Harmondsworth: Penguin, 1976])

Project

Find out what your friends and relatives think are the causes of poverty. Using the list provided above and any other reasons that the class has come up with go out and survey at least five relatives and friends. Bring your results to class next time and compare them with your classmates.

Debate

Divide yourselves into two teams (For and Against) and brainstorm as many arguments as you can. Then either split up your arguments among the team and each side take turns presenting and defending your case, or pair off with a member of the opposing team and argue it out face to face. Argue either for or against the following statement.

> Poverty is a persistent problem, and nothing that we as individuals can do will improve the plight of the poor.

Teacher's Notes and Answer Key

Inside a Third World City

Task 1. c is the best answer.

Task 2. c is the best answer.

Task 3. shanties = small, badly built houses; *rags* = old, worn-out clothes; a *cripple* = someone who cannot walk; *ramshackle* = badly made and in need of repair; *shameless* = with no concern for one's bad behavior; *mug* = rob with violence

Task 4.

a. A cripple draws sidewalk pictures to collect money to pay for an operation (or a red-faced woman coughs . . . and holds out her hand for money)
b. and the uncaring rich . . . are so unbelievably shameless that . . .
c. lawyers and businesspeople . . . pay their peasants so little that they have to leave for the cities
d. Above all they rob, mug, and terrorize the middle classes.

Task 5. Students should be able to think of more than the following, which is just what is stated in the text. *Homes*—rich: smart suburbs (plus huge country estates); poor: shanties of wood and cardboard, slums without light, roads or water. *Jobs*—rich: lawyers, businesspeople, landlords, landowners, secretaries, bank employees; poor: beggars, street artists, rubbish collectors, thieves. *Food and drink*: rich: whiskey; poor: leftovers. *Schooling*: no specific information, but the young poor learn survival skills on the streets. *Health care*: obviously everyone has to pay, including the cripple, but who will have health insurance?

Task 6. Again, these are open-ended questions. Answers should contain some reference to the high rents and lack of work in the cities and to the need to pay for *everything* from medical care to empty bottles. As for improving the future of the poor, answers may range from the charitable to the revolutionary.

Inside an English City

Task 1. 3, 2, 4, 1

Task 2. Suitable questions would be as follows (many others are possible). What do their nicknames refer to? What was Sunderland famous for? How are they affected by the consumer spectacle around them? How do they relieve the boredom of their lives? What do they usually talk about? What kinds of TV programs do they watch?

Task 3. Hopelessness: aimless, unwanted, wasted, unsatisfying, lack of worth; *threatening behavior:* thrust at, taunt, despises, humiliates, destroys; *control:* enforced, locked into, subordination, captivity, keep in place. The effect is to *reinforce* the writer's main point—that the boys have no control over their hopeless lives and therefore react with threats of violence.

Task 4. b, c, and d.

Task 5. O, O, F, O, F, and O (though some may argue that the second and third statements are F and O respectively).

Task 7. This is open-ended. Students should at least come up with educational opportunities, moving to another town, self-education (libraries, etc.).

Fluency Activities

Information gap. Again, this is an open-ended task. Some possible answers include the following. *Similarities:* no work, no money, they get poorer while the rich get richer, petty theft such as picking pockets, their poverty leads to violence. *Differences*: the Sunderland boys need money for excitement and escape, not for basic needs like food; they fantasize a lot about suicide and have very low self-esteem, while the *gamines* are much more street smart, using their skills (e.g., singing and begging) to stay alive.

Evaluation 1. There is a difference between absolute poverty—the basic necessities of life—and relative poverty, which varies from country to country and place to place.

Evaluation 2. Many experts believe that lack of jobs, lack of goods to sell, and the distribution of land are the main causes. All of the other items except laziness are contributory factors, though there is dispute about the relevance of population factors.

Guesstimates. Rich capitalist countries have 20% of the population and 65% of the income, the ex-Soviet bloc has 10% of the population and 15% of the income, but the Third World has 70% of the population and 20% of the income. (Data from Tony Garrett, "Society Today," *New Society,* 30 May 1985, ii.)

Creative Thinking. This is a completely open-ended activity. The underpinning idea is that resources are poorly allocated. Can you think of what a reallocation of resources would mean—globally, nationally, and personally?

Unit 10
Guys 'n' Dolls

Woman's Work Is Never Done

Prereading

Which of these jobs are more suitable for men and which for women?

office cleaner	school cook	dressmaker
child care worker	supermarket cashier	

In groups think about and discuss your reasons for deciding as you did.

Reading

Look at task 1 below and then read through the text quickly, without using a dictionary.

In the case of women's work, there is an undeniable contradiction. Women's work in the family remains essential; indeed, the smaller the family unit gets, the more we hear about **its** preservation. Meanwhile, the expansion of production means there are more goods to sell and new kinds of jobs to be done. The reduction of housework time, combined with contraception, has meant that many more married women have become available for work. Woman-power has thus become an essential part of commodity production. By making use of both husband's and wife's labor, capitalism has been able to allow the family unit a higher income; but **this** also means that most women have been left with a double load of work: in the home and outside it.

Despite capitalism's current dependence on married women as a permanent and essential part of the workforce, employers still often behave as if they were doing women a favor by employing them. **They** still act as if women should somehow be grateful for the chance to be exploited. **This** is particularly ironic when we look at the jobs that are considered "women's work." The only factor these jobs really have in common is low pay, which means the profit that capitalism takes from women is direct and crude.

Originally "women's work" was housework. The kinds of tasks done in the home remained women's jobs when work and home became separated. Despite many changes, some industries still retain **this.** Textile and clothing industries still have a large female labor force; food processing and catering are still largely done by women. The concept of women's work means that certain skills—such as cleaning, cooking, or child care—are considered "natural" for females and so are not highly valued in money terms. Indeed, the more closely work resembles housework the less it has the status of "real" work, even when it is both dirty and physically tiring. Cleaning is a clear example of **this.** The low pay of cleaners, both in offices and factories, represents the money value that capitalism puts on housework when it appears in industry.

Similarly, many women in supermarkets are shelf-fillers, which involves considerable lifting, pushing, and carrying. As long as work resembles housework, the fact that it is heavy doesn't matter. Thus the notion of women's work as an extension of a woman's role in the family serves to conceal that much of this work is hard and dirty; it also enables employers to retain paternalistic forms of control over women workers and demand more labor from them, which is not even reflected in the pay envelope.

Task 1

Match these paragraph summaries to the four paragraphs in the text.

[ ] Employers do not recognize the value of their female workers and consistently underpay them.

[ ] Many hard and dirty jobs are considered natural for women, simply because they resemble housework.

[ ] Capitalism needs women's cheap labor, without freeing them from their work in the home.

[ ] The concept of "women's work" is a method for (male) employers to control women.

Task 2

Write down all the technical words and phrases from the text connected with the economy.

Adapted from S. Rowbotham, *Woman's Consciousness, Man's World* (Harmondsworth: Penguin), 81–90.

Task 3

What do the following words printed in **bold** in the text refer to?

its (para. 1)	this (para. 2)
this (para. 1)	this (para. 3)
they (para. 2)	this (para. 3)

Task 4

Match these words from the text with their definitions.

contraception	used unfairly for profit
commodity	protective but like a dominant father
exploited	birth control
catering	something made and sold for profit
paternalistic	providing and serving food

Task 5

Which of the following phrases best describes the content of the text? Why?

balanced and fair
biased and unreasonable
informative but one-sided
emotional and lacking in facts

Who's That Man?

Prereading

Which of these men do you think looks the most masculine? Why do you think so?

Reading

Look at task 1 below and then read through the text quickly, without using a dictionary.

When I was thirteen, two boys approached me at school, they said they were going to ask me an important question. "Was I," they inquired, "a heterosexual?" "No," I said. That was the reply they had expected. "Then you must be a **queer**," was their response. I felt thrown into panic, because, though I hadn't understood what the word meant, I assumed that sexual labels were for sexual **deviance.** It's an incident about **naïveté,** but it also reflects the assumption that "normal sexuality" is both beyond question and beyond description; women may be sexual beings, but men are just **fellows,** the **guys**.

Heterosexual men have taken refuge in this idea that our sexual identities are absolute. Heterosexual masculinity shifts its problems and anxieties onto the image of the **compliant** female, . . . and the **perverted** homosexual. Today this masculine myth is being sufficiently questioned to drag it into view. The representation of different masculinities has produced two idealized images that correspond to the **repressed** and the public meanings of masculinity: what I'll call the New Man and the Retributive Man respectively.

Retributive Man represents the struggle to reassert a traditional masculinity, a tough, independent authority. The classic figure is Rambo. He confronts a world gone soft, pacified by traitors and cowards, dishonorable feminized men. It is a world that has **disrupted** his notions of manhood and honor. He advertises a destructive machismo as the solution to men's problems. He represents a belief that the individual man has only himself to rely on for his own, and for national, salvation. Both the filmic images and the reality represent a masculinity in crisis.

In contrast, New Man is an expression of the repressed body of masculinity; it is an attempt to express masculine emotional and sexual life. The current crop of magazines for men is hooking in to the new narcissism of men. Pictures of young, male models are portrayed in passive, "feminized" poses. The heterosexual male reader is confronted with a challenge, the new object of his gaze is another man. We are invited to take pleasure from these male bodies and the clothes they wear. Similarly, the changing face of fatherhood: the new liberalized image of men pushing buggies, attending births, and **cuddling** babies in public without fear of shame or ridicule has been taken up and encouraged by the media. Yet there is little tangible evidence that men are now more involved in the care of their children. Advertising agencies are loathe to figure the New Man in food- and shopping-related ads, because these are areas where, they believe, women are still predominant.

The disruption to our sexual identity has produced a new flexibility in masculinity. But what hasn't happened is any attempt to address this potential for change. There is no sexual politics that engages heterosexual men, that can connect with the market created identities and argue for new, democratic forms of heterosexuality and **eroticism.** While the women's magazines regularly feature women's interrogation of masculinity, magazines aimed at men studiously ignore taking up such concerns.

How we look at other men, how we touch them, the **stance** and rigidity of our bodies, the ways we speak to each other and the subjects we discuss, what feelings we show and the kinds of behavior we exhibit—all these are codes that are used to **police** men and that we employ to protect ourselves. Our relationships with each other are diminished by doubt and insecurity. I can remember all those times at school, the retribution and punishment we handed out to boys who were different, fat boys and **effeminate** boys. As we grew older we learned to keep our heads down and **follow the pack.** We wouldn't have dared to admit a **longing** for another boy, better to hit or **humiliate** him instead.

Adapted from Jonathan Rutherford, "Who's That Man," in *Male Order—Unwrapping Masculinity*, Rowena Chapman and Jonathan Rutherford (London: Lawrence & Wishart Ltd., 1988), 22–60.

Task 1

Which of these is the best summary of the text?

a. Heterosexual men, both those who identify with Retributive Man and those who identify with New Man, are now taking a more flexible approach to their masculinity in order to accommodate the views of women and gays.
b. Heterosexual masculinity, which has for so long considered itself beyond question, is now being represented by a variety of competing models; however, most men's awareness has not yet reached a level where real changes in their relationships with others can occur.
c. Because of the growing influence of sexual politics, the images of masculinity are changing, and the traditional Rambo-type model is no longer adequate in a society that demands a softer, more passive man, who can be democratic in his relationships with others.

Task 2

Which of these statements are true [T], which are false [F], and which are not answered in the text [NA]?

[ ] The writer is a homosexual.
[ ] Traditional male sexuality does not see its own problems and anxieties.
[ ] All men can be classified as either New Men or Retributive Men.
[ ] The New Man does not in fact take more part in child care than Retributive Man.
[ ] The New Men's magazines are not interested in sexual politics.
[ ] Men's desire to be seen as "normal" leads to shallower relationships with others.

Task 3

Note down key words that describe the characteristics of New Man and Retributive Man.

New Man	Retributive Man

Task 4

Rewrite the first sentences of paragraphs 2, 3, 4, and 5 so that they are easier to understand.

paragraph 2. ______________________________

____

paragraph 3. ______________________________

____

paragraph 4. ______________________________

____

paragraph 5. ______________________________

____

Task 5

Look at the words in **bold** in the text. Circle the ones that you do not know. Which of the words that you do not know prevent you from understanding something important in the text? Find out what they mean, preferably without using a dictionary.

Task 6

Discuss the following points in small groups.

a. In paragraph 2 the text says the "masculine myth is being sufficiently questioned to drag it into view." Who is questioning it?
b. Who do you think is creating the new images of masculinity?
c. This text was written with British society in mind. Are the same images of masculinity popular in your culture or are there different ones?

Fluency Activities

Sharing Ideas

Imagine you had been born the opposite sex. How would your life, past, present, and future, be different? List your ideas.

Compare what you have written in small, preferably mixed-sex, groups.

Personal Information

Ask your partner the following questions and note down his/her answers.

When you were five to ten years old:

What did you want to be when you grew up?
What toys did you play with?
Which family member did you feel closest to?
Which cartoon characters did you like best?
What sports did you play at school?

Compare your answers in small mixed-sex groups. What does this tell you about how your concept of masculinity/femininity was formed?

Try It for Yourself

Form small groups if possible of equal numbers of men and women. First the women teach the men how to walk, sit down, and bend down to pick something up like a woman. The men must *perform* the actions until they can do them adequately. Then the men teach the women to do the same actions like a man.

Now discuss the following.

How did it feel to move like a member of the opposite sex?
In what way did it feel different from your usual way of moving?
What does this tell you about the everyday roles of women and men?

Dis/Agreement

Your teacher will dictate a short paragraph. Write it down as it is ONLY IF you agree with what it says. If at any point you disagree, change what the teacher says to reflect your own point of view before writing.

In groups, read out your dictations, one by one, allowing other group members to comment on any changes you have made.

Project

Look out for advertisements that show the following.

people conforming to stereotyped gender roles
people breaking gender stereotypes

Bring some to show to your classmates.

Debate

Divide yourselves into two teams (For and Against) and brainstorm as many arguments as you can. Then either split up your arguments among the team and each side take turns presenting and defending your case, or pair off with a member of the opposing team and argue it out face to face. Argue either for or against the following statement.

> Wives and husbands should share ALL housekeeping and child care equally and have equal duty to earn income.

Teacher's Notes and Answer Key

Woman's Work Is Never Done

Prereading. This is an open-ended activity. Obviously both men and women are capable of doing all the jobs listed, but since students are asked to choose, most will. Their reasons for deciding suitability will probably highlight the stereotyped nature of gender roles: for example, for men—physical strength or responsibility (office cleaning, cashier—though in supermarkets this is usually done by women working part-time); for women—caring and nurturing or feminine interest (child care worker, school cook, and dressmaker). In fact, in industrialized countries, these jobs are mostly done by women, because they resemble work done in the home and are low-paid and/or part-time work.

Task 1. 2, 3, 1, 4

Task 2. work, production, goods, commodity, labor, capitalism, income, workforce, employer, low pay, profit, industries, money value

Task 3. *its* = the family unit; *this* = using both husband's and wife's labor; *they* = employers; *this* = the way employers act; *this* = the idea that women's work resembles housework; *this* = "housework"-type work doesn't have the status of "real" work

Task 4. *contraception* = birth control; *commodity* = something made and sold for profit; *exploited* = used unfairly for profit; *catering* = providing and serving food; *paternalistic* = protective but like a dominant father

Task 5. We think 3 is the best answer.

Who's That Man?

Prereading. another open-ended activity designed to focus on stereotyped views of masculinity

Task 1. We think b is the best answer.

Task 2. NA, T, F, TA, T, T

Task 3. Retributive Man: traditional, tough, independent, confrontational, destructive, machismo, self-reliant, Ramboesque
New Man: emotionally and sexually expressive, narcissistic, open to the avant-garde, liberated fathers

Task 4. Suitable answers might be: *paragraph 2:* Heterosexual men like to think that gender roles are fixed; *paragraph 3:* Retributive Man has a tough, independent image, the traditional man; *paragraph 4:* New Man has a more emotional and sexual image; *paragraph 5:* The changes in our ideas about sex roles have made men more flexible.

Task 6. This is an open-ended task, but possible answers include the following.

a. the writer, people studying gender roles, women's magazines, gay men and lesbians, feminists
b. men's magazines, the media, some advertisers
c. Obviously everyone's answers will be different.

Fluency Activities

Sharing Ideas. This is an open-ended activity. Try to get students to go beyond the obvious superficial differences.

Try It for Yourself. Allow at least twenty minutes for this activity. Men are usually surprised at how controlled, restrictive, and tiring moving as a woman is, whereas women usually find a greater sense of freedom and power when they move like men. (This activity was taught to us by Randi Donnis.)

Dis/Agreement. Dictate the following passage, giving students time to consider and write.

> Men and women are physically different and think differently: men are logical while women rely on emotion. This is why women are better at bringing up children and men are natural leaders in business and politics. It also explains why the husband's role is to protect and support his family, even though many men now allow their wives to go out to work and in return help to look after the home.

In the discussion stage, encourage students to ask why others modified the text in the ways they did. This is good preparation for the debate.
(This is based on a dictation exercise learned from Mario Rinvolucri at the JALT annual conference, Kobe, Japan, 1988.)

Grateful acknowledgment is made to the following authors, publishers, and journals for permission to reprint previously published materials.

Alfred A. Knopf, Inc., and David Higham Associates for excerpt from *A Secret Country* by John Pilger. Copyright © 1988 by John Pilger. Reprinted by permission of Alfred A. Knopf, Inc., and David Higham Associates.

Alyson Publications, Inc., for excerpt from *Reflections of a Rock Lobster* by Aaron Fricke (Boston: Alyson Publications, 1985). Copyright © 1981 Alyson Publications, Inc. Reprinted with permission.

A M Heath for excerpt from *The Want Makers* by Eric Clark (Harmondsworth: Penguin Books, 1990). Copyright © Eric Clark. Reprinted with permission.

BBC Worldwide for excerpt from "Racial Equality at Work" by David Henshaw, in the *Listener,* 1 July 1982.

Camden Press Ltd. and Tim Lobstein for excerpt from *Fast Food Facts* by Tim Lobstein (London: Camden Press Ltd., 1988). Copyright © 1988 Camden Press Ltd. Reprinted with permission.

CBS News Archives for "Can Older Workers Save America?" by Doug Tunnell, broadcast May 1991. Reprinted with permission.

Christian Aid for adaptation of "The Trading Game." © Christian Aid, P.O. Box 100, London SW1 7RT. Reprinted with permission.

Christian Science Monitor for "Organic Farming Puts Down Roots" by Elizabeth A. Brown, in *Christian Science Monitor,* 17 January 1989. Reprinted by permission from the *Christian Science Monitor,* © 1989 The Christian Science Publishing Society. All rights reserved.

The *Guardian* for "Murder in the Rainforests" by Tim Radford, in the *Guardian,* 5 January 1989; and for "Back in the Sixties . . . No longer doped I chose my life" by Susie Pritchard, in the *Guardian,* September 1989, the Guardian © 1989. Reprinted with permission.

The *Guardian* and Paulette Farsides for "Fear of the Naturals" by Paulette Farsides, in the *Guardian,* 11 January 1991. Reprinted with permission.

Paul Harrison for excerpt from *Inside the Third World,* 3d ed., by Paul Harrison (Harmondsworth: Penguin, 1993). Reprinted with permission.

Lawrence & Wishart Ltd for excerpt from "Who's That Man" by Jonathan Rutherford, in *Male Order—Unwrapping Masculinity* by Rowena Chapman and Jonathan Rutherford (London: Lawrence & Wishart Ltd., 1988). Reprinted with permission.

Le Monde for adaptation of "Bangladesh's Penny Bank Gives Hope to the Rural Poor" by Roland-Pierre Paringaux, in *Guardian Weekly, Le Monde* section, 30 April 1989; and for article by Christian de Brie in *Le Monde Diplomatique,* October 1989, translated and reprinted in *Guardian Weekly* 141, no. 20 (19 November 1989). Reprinted with permission.

New Democrat International for article by Peter Hughes in *New Democrat International,* November/December 1990, 4–5.

Vance Packard for excerpt from *The Hidden Persuaders* by Vance Packard (Harmondsworth: Penguin Books, 1957 and 1981). Reprinted with permission.

Penguin Books USA Inc. for excerpts from *Cut Stones and Crossroads* by Ronald Wright, copyright © 1984 by Ronald Wright, used by permission of Viking Penguin, a division of Penguin Books USA Inc.; and for excerpt from *Woman's Consciousness, Man's World* by Sheila Rowbotham (London: Penguin Books, 1973), copyright © 1973 Sheila Rowbotham, reprinted with permission.

Quartet Books for excerpt from *Unemployment* by Jeremy Seabrook (London: Quartet Books, 1982). Reprinted with permission.

Lucie Young for "The Incredible Ageing Woman" by Lucie Young, in the *Guardian,* 1 August 1989. Reprinted with permission.

Special acknowledgment is made to the following companies for use of their advertisements: ACTIONAID, Bristol-Myers Company Limited, Coal Products Limited, DDD Limited, McCann Erickson and Ellesse, Heublein Incorporated, Hitachi (UK), ISDD Publishers, Kellogg's Company of Great Britain Limited, Kleinwort Benson, Lever Brothers Limited and Peter Rauter, Rimmel Chicogo, Seal Incorporated, Sime Health and GJR Advertising, Taunton Cider Company, Thorntons, Vauxhall Motors.

Every effort has been made to trace the ownership of all copyrighted material in this book and to obtain permission for its use.